FOR AL, HELEN AND RON WITH LOVE

THE STRUCTURE OF THE MISSIONARY CALL TO THE SANDWICH ISLANDS 1790-1830

Sojourners Among Strangers

Editorial Inquiries:

Mellen Research University Press
534 Pacific Avenue
San Francisco, California 94133

Order Fulfillment:

The Edwin Mellen Press
Box 450
Lewiston, New York 14092

THE STRUCTURE OF THE MISSIONARY CALL TO THE SANDWICH ISLANDS 1790-1830

Sojourners Among Strangers

Sandra Wagner-Wright

Distinguished Dissertations Series
Volume 2

MELLEN RESEARCH UNIVERSITY PRESS
San Francisco

BV
3680
·H3
W34
1990

Library of Congress Cataloging-in-Publication Data

This book has been registered with the Library of Congress.

This is volume 2 in the continuing series
Distinguished Dissertations Series
Volume 2 ISBN 0-7734-9938-5
DDS Series ISBN 0-7734-9944-X

Printed in the United States of America

TABLE OF CONTENTS

FOREWORD

Two historians and a sociologist have written letters in support of Sojourners Among Strangers. All have felt that it represents a significant contribution to the study of missionaries, because it places the missionaries to the Sandwich Islands within their theological and cultural context.

Dr. Cedric Cowing is Associate Professor of History at the University of Hawaii at Manoa located at Honolulu, Hawaii. His specialty is United States colonial history.

I can only be enthusiastic about the decision of the Mellen Press to publish "Sojourners Among Strangers" in its Distinguished Dissertation Series. Prof. Wagner-Wright has made an important contribution to the missionary literature. She is able to offer many words of the missionaries themselves--material not previously available--that makes it possible for the reader to make his own assessment of motivations.

The strength of the manuscript for me is the linking of the ideas and experiences of the missionaries in Hawaii with the Puritan heritage of the colonial period, and the connections she makes with the then current modifications of that theological heritage, i.e., the "disinterested benevolence" of the Edwardean New Divinity school.

"Sojourners Among Strangers" will be especially useful here in Hawaii in showing more clearly what the motivations of the missionaries really were. Too often their theology has been caricatured or oversimplified. Of course there is great interest in missionaries throughout the Pacific and this book will find a variety of readers from a number of disciplines. I look forward to seeing it in print.

Dr. Stewart Firth is Associate Professor of History at Macquarie University in Sydney, Australia. His specialty is Pacific history.

Dr. Wagner-Wright of the History Department at the University of Hawaii at Hilo has asked me to offer my evaluation of the scholarly contribution which her book manuscript makes to the study of Pacific history.

I should first explain my own qualifications to offer an opinion. I am an Australian scholar who has specialised in Pacific history since first teaching at the University of Papua New Guinea in the late 1960s; my Oxford doctorate focussed on Pacific Islands colonial history; I was an Associate Professor in Pacific History at the University of Hawaii in 1982-83; and last year I spent six months as a Visiting Professor at the Center for Pacific Island Studies at the University of Hawaii. I have published a number of books in the field and I am book review editor of the Journal of Pacific History.

With only a few exceptions, historians of Pacific missions have been divided into two broad camps over the last twenty years: the pietistic and the reductionist. The first school of thought proceeds from Christian assumptions, the second reduces everything to other, less noble motivations, psycho-sexual ones for example. Neither offers a satisfactory explanation of what drove the missionaries to their task.

The unique contribution made by "Sojourners Among Strangers" is that it puts theological concerns back in the middle of the picture, where they belong, without becoming a confessional or pietistic history. The manuscript evokes a whole way of thinking about the world that is no longer central to American culture, but was very much at its centre in the early nineteenth century, at least in New England. In this sense, the writer of "Sojourners Among Strangers" must be seen as being in the best tradition of historians who take the sympathetic evocation of the past as their primary task, and who endeavour to free themselves from the assumptions of the present.

From the viewpoint of the Pacific historian, the achievement of Dr. Wagner-Wright is to remind

us of the wider theological world with which the
Pacific Islands came into contact in the early
nineteenth century, and which has influenced them
so profoundly ever since. Perhaps no part of the
world has been so thoroughly Christianised as the
Islands; so it is important to know in detail about
the varieties of Christianity that came with the
missionaries. The history of Christianity is
central to the history of the Pacific; and what Dr.
Wagner-Wright has done is to demonstrate the
theological link between New England in the early
nineteenth century and the Christianity of the
Pacific.

For these reasons I have no hesitation in
saying that "Sojourners Among Strangers" represents
a considerable scholarly contribution to the field
of Pacific history.

Dr. Jeffrey L. Crane is Associate Professor of
Sociology and Chair of the Social Sciences Division at
the University of Hawaii at Hilo in Hilo, Hawaii. Dr.
Crane has a long-standing interest in missionary
evangelism in Hawaii.

Professor Sandra Wagner-Wright's monograph,
Sojourners Among Strangers: The Structure of the
Missionary Call to the Sandwich Islands 1790-1830,
is an important contribution to Hawaiian history and
the social history of religion in the US. This
highly readable text will probably not find an
immediately sympathetic audience since Dr. Wagner-
Wright has dared to challenge conventional thinking
regarding missionary movements and impacts.

In examining existing literature in this area,
especially that pertaining to the Hawaiian
missionary experience, social historians and other
social scientists have tended to advance one or two
interpretations. First, and perhaps the most
popular, are those works which paint the
missionaries and their various missions as
colonialism. The second, and not necessarily
exclusive, approach has been to cast the cultures
and social structures of native peoples in terms of
decay predicated upon either contact with other
cultures or internal weaknesses borne of
transitional periods. In this latter, and very
paternalistic, scenario the missionaries are
frequently viewed as zealots, idealists, misguided

cultural colonialists who foist their world-views
upon people hardly in positions to resist.

Dr. Wagner-Wright challenges these prevailing
accounts by insisting that the missionaries cannot
be understood apart from their faith and cultural
experiences. In essence hers is a sociology of
knowledge portrait of the missionaries in Hawaii.
As such, it proffers insights and interpretations
that are both novel and significant. Moreover,
unlike the two model driven approaches briefly
sketched above, Dr. Wagner-Wright's work makes
extensive use of the missionaries' own writing - and
thereby furnishes the reader with a first-hand view
into the fears, joys, doubts, and conflicts
perceived and experienced by the missionaries
themselves.

Weaving together the notions of theology,
conversion experiences, institution, and individual,
Dr. Wagner-Wright crafts a picture of the
missionaries that is both novel and informative.
Without attributing economic, cultural, or political
imperialism to their intentions, the missionaries
are depicted as people living out their biographies
and cultures in a social context which did not
readily accommodate their world-view. Dr. Wagner-
Wright argues convincingly that biographical factors
(e.g., conversion experiences and individual
expectations), grounded in an ideological framework
(i.e., theology), conjoined with institutional
factors (e.g., the American Board of Commissioners
for Foreign Missions) to shape and determine the
missionary experience in Hawaii. In the final
analysis what Dr. Wagner-Wright produces is a first-
rate social historical account of Hawaii's
missionaries.

This work will have appeal to those scholars
and students of early nineteenth century American
history, the history of New England and Hawaii, and
US religious history in general. It will be
especially attractive to those scholars who are
interested in reexamining the conventional wisdom
surrounding the entire phenomenon of religious
missionaries.

Sojourners Among Strangers represents a departure
from the usual depiction of missionaries to Hawaii,
because it presents these evangelists within their own

cultural context. It is not merely a collection of personal biographies, but an investigation into the New England religious environment that produced so many young adults willing to commit their lives to a vocation that promised no gain in either this world or the next.

INTRODUCTION

Mission is part and parcel of the American myth. The terminology has changed over time, from Christian evangelism to Save the Children, but the idea of spreading American culture and largesse looms large in our psyche. The Puritans laid the foundation for such an altruistic trait with the founding of the "city on a hill" in 1630. Its purpose was not the material gain of the participants, although in time they did prosper. Rather, the immigrants hoped New England would serve as a beacon for the Church of England, calling Anglican backsliders to the Reformed view of Scripture and congregational polity. After the disappointments of the English Civil War and the Protectorate (1640-1660), the Puritans concluded that a beacon was not enough, that a new society based on Calvinist precepts was in order.

Calvinist theology required selfless devotion from the Elect, the continual calling of the unregenerate, and constant efforts toward personal salvation. Identifying the unregenerate was a bit like identifying one's neighbor in the parable of the Good Samaritan. The unregenerate were the unbelievers in every culture. They were the unchurched, the Anglicans, the "popish" Catholics, the Quakers, the Native Americans. The selected object of Puritan missionary efforts was not among those who heard the truth and rejected it, though they were urged to attend church. The object of New England missionary interests was the Native American. Later, it would be the Asian, the Turk, the Sandwich

Islander. All would be approached with the same basic methodology.

Calvinist theology provided an effective intellectual framework for missionary work both in New England and throughout the world. Not all missionaries were Calvinist, but without a strong theology such as Calvinism both the mission and the missionary suffered from a lack of purpose. Throughout history theology has provided the self-definition of the missionary and his or her work. It has motivated young adults, and sometimes older ones as well, to embark on a formidable task. And once in the field, theology has enabled the missionary to identify candidates for conversion.

Institutional structures provide the practical means of getting the missionary into the field. The institution recruits, selects and trains the missionary candidates. It handles logistics, collects donations, keeps the cause of mission before the public eye and provides the link between the missionary and the Christian world. The American Board of Commissioners for Foreign Missions founded in 1810 provided such services to its members. It was the pinnacle of the voluntary societies that gave structure to the Second Great Awakening (1790-1840). Contemporary theology demanded active proof of conversion, usually demonstrated by participation in a voluntary society. Foreign missionaries provided the premier example of selfless devotion to God's kingdom. Any association with that work made the Christian at home a vicarious member of the missionary family.

Missionaries, then, are the implementators of both theology and institution. In the person of the missionary, the theoretical and the practical merge. It is the missionary who undergoes conviction and conversion, who receives the call to mission, who perceives what that call entails and acts upon it. It is the missionary who experiences doubts and assurances, elation and despair. He or she is the flesh and blood of it all.

Twentieth century historians have been quite hard on missionaries, most often depicting them as the vanguard of imperialism, economic adventurers or misguided idealists. Clifton Philips' groundbreaking work on the subject (Protestant America and the Pagan World) paints the missionaries in a decidedly destructive light with no attempt to understand the basis of their behavior. John Andrew (Rebuilding the Christian Commonwealth) is concerned only with institutional structure; the participants are incidental. And Patricia Grimshaw's recently published work (Paths of Duty) is a chronicle of women who came to Hawaii during the nineteenth century with an eye to feminist issues. None of these studies (or others like them in the field) gives an accurate picture of the missionary enterprise, because none looks at the totality of the missionary effort.

The present study attempts to look at all the forces that influenced the call and establishment of the mission field in the Sandwich Islands. Missionaries do not exist in a vacuum. They are the product of their regional environment and they rely on the continued support and commitment of their countrymen and women. That network was an important aspect of missionary life.

This study is limited to the first two companies of missionaries to the Sandwich Islands (1820 and 1823, respectively), because these individuals were the product of a specific type of Calvinist theology. Jonathan Edwards and the New Divinity men envisioned a conversion experience which so merged the will of the Christian and the Creator that the former would cheerfully descend to Hell if that were necessary for God's plan. Theirs was a patriarchal theology based on an understanding of Scripture that was linked to New England culture. This linkage meant that missionaries were not only charged to spread the Gospel, but also the cultural mores necessary for its "correct" understanding.

Previous histories of missionary endeavors have either been done by religiously-oriented historians who credited the success or failure of a mission to the faith of the participants or by revisionists who interpreted missionary activities in a completely secular light. Neither is correct.

There is a saying in Hawaii that the missionaries came to do good and stayed to do well. It reflects the public perception that the missionaries were responsible for the Americanization of Hawaii. When I began my research, I expected to find that the missionaries to Hawaii came for much the same reason that other New Englanders were migrating west, to improve their economic position. However, as I read their journals and investigated their background, I discovered that the vast majority of members of the first two companies came to Hawaii as a result of their faith. Furthermore, the mission church in Hawaii excommunicated one couple, Dr. and Mrs. Thomas Holman, because their motives were less than altruistic. While it is true that Calvinist missionaries insisted on cultural change, they did so from a theological rather than a market motivation. Thus, it is impossible to understand missionaries apart from their theology, because that is the basis of their sub-culture. This history restores theology to its formative position while also considering the milieu of New England culture in the early nineteenth century. For those individuals who eventually joined the American Board, it was a culture permeated by a Calvinist God.

    This work would not have been possible without the encouragement and assistance of numerous individuals. I would like to thank Mary Jane Knight and Lela Goodell, librarians at the Research Library at the Hawaiian Mission Children's Society in Honolulu; Barbara Dunn executive secretary of the Hawaiian Historical Society in Honolulu and Christine Lothian, librarian at the Lyman House Memorial Museum in Hilo, Hawaii. These individuals cheerfully and patiently introduced me to the intricacies of their collections.   I am grateful to those institutions for permission to use their materials in this publication. I would also like to thank the patient ladies at the Interlibrary Loan Office in Hamilton Library at the University of Hawaii at Manoa who kindly processed innumerable requests for material.

    Numerous individuals read and commented on various parts of the manuscript during its formative stages. Cedric Cowing, Stewart Firth, Judith Hughes, Brig Lal, Robert R. Locke, Martin E. Marty, I. A. Newby and Sara Sohmer offered particularly useful commentary on the emerging product.

    Last, but far from least, I would like to thank my husband, Ron, for his enthusiasm and patience during the final revisions. He never doubted the project would reach a successful conclusion, and that missionary ghosts would finally disappear from the dinner table.

    To all of these individuals, and others who helped along the way, I say mahalo nui loa!

III

    Sojourners Among Strangers is a profile of people who did much to found modern Hawaii. They set the tone for nineteenth and early twentieth century Hawaii. My current research project, "Say Aloha With Macadamia Nuts: The History of the Macadamia Nut Industry in Hawaii 1881-1981," looks at the development of what is now Hawaii's third largest agricultural industry. It is a new departure for me in every way, because it deals with an enterprise established during my lifetime and with sources I look for in orchards rather than libraries. But the men and women in this industry are also pioneers, and their efforts will impact on the Hawaii of the twenty-first century. The formative years of any enterprise are the most exciting, and this will be the first published history of an industry which has become a symbol of Hawaii.

IV

History is more than facts and events; it is the story of people. We understand history only as well as we can understand the people involved. It is their ideology, motivations and aspirations which create the tapestry that historians find so fascinating.

Sojourners Among Strangers is the story of the first two companies of missionaries to the Sandwich Islands, but it is also the story of their New England ancestors. The individuals introduced in these pages are part of the warp and weft of history. I have not always agreed with their policies or the results of those policies, but I have come to appreciate why and how these missionaries arrived at their decisions. I have tried to share that knowledge with a minimum of imperfections, but my success at telling this story is for the reader to judge.

Hilo, Hawaii

May, 1990

CHAPTER I

ACCEPTANCE OF THE GREAT COMMISSION

"Go ye therefore, and teach all nations,
baptizing them in the name of the Father, and
of the Son, and of the Holy Ghost: teaching
them to observe all things whatsoever I have
commanded you: and, lo, I am with you alway,
even unto the end of the world. Amen.
(Matthew 28:19-20)

These words represent the last commandment of Jesus
and the impetus for the Christian church. Reception of
the new teaching was not enough; action was required.
Evangelism and missionary activity became the order of
the day, beginning with the itinerant efforts of the
Apostle Paul and continuing into our present age.

The Great Commission, however, is only a directive.
It describes what must be done, but not how the task
should be accomplished or by whom. This lack of
specifics resulted in as many approaches to evangelism
as there are Christian theologies, some experiencing
more success than others.

The Reformed tradition of Calvinism comprises a
theology that not only served to bind its adherents
together in their search for salvation but also provided
a strong motivation for missionary activity. Calvinists
became particularly active in preaching to unbelievers
whether of their own or another culture during the late
eighteenth and early nineteenth centuries. This was a
time of evangalism, revivalism and millennial
expectations in both the United States and Great
Britain.

American Congregationalists and Presbyterians, as a natural outgrowth of their Calvinist theology, founded the American Board of Commissioners for Foreign Missions (hereinafter referred to as the American Board) in 1810. That institution sponsored work in Asia, the Middle East, frontier America and the Sandwich Islands. It recruited missionaries and kept the cause in the public eye through periodicals, voluntary support groups and speaking tours. It provided linkage between the workers in foreign fields and the faithful at home.

The workers in foreign fields, however, are something of an enigma. From a twentieth century perspective it is difficult to appreciate the religiosity of early nineteenth century American society. The modern historian would prefer to attribute nineteenth century missionary activity to twentieth century "isms" -- capitalism, imperialism, perhaps even idealism. Such is not the case. Early nineteenth century American missionaries left kith and kin in order to preach to unbelievers. They left because they felt a call from God to serve Him in foreign climes. They left without hope of repatriation or worldly gain or even of personal salvation. Those accepting the call to mission did so with the expectation of martyrdom and the hope of God's kingdom.

The first two companies of missionaries to the Sandwich Islands provide the evidence of these assertions. Twenty-seven individuals received the baton of the Reformed tradition and volunteered for service with the American Board. Like modern astronauts and their dependence on NASA, these missionaries could not have participated in the great work without the extensive support provided by a network of voluntary societies, and a belief in the reasonableness of their actions.[1]

II

The concept implied by the term missionary changes to suit the historical moment. The idea entertained by those embarking for the Sandwich Islands in 1819 and 1822, respectively, was an outgrowth of European traditions pertaining to cultural "others" and Puritan efforts among the American Indians. The work of John Eliot and David Brainerd enjoyed a wide readership during the Second Great Awakening (1790-1840). Eliot supplied a definition and methodology for the work while Brainerd exemplified the romantic ideal of the selfless missionary forsaking health and all earthly comforts to be of service to God and His creatures.

On a more practical level, theology and experience offered guidelines on discerning a call and acting upon it. Articles in periodicals such as the Panoplist informed readers of the work being done in Tahiti, Asia and Africa by the London Missionary Society. The faith requirements of a missionary were clearly set out, though practical aspects were not as evident. The literate Christian public respected a foreign missionary in much the same way that medieval society venerated those entering the monastic life. Surely, these individuals must be among the saved.

Such assurance, however, was completely lacking for the individuals most directly involved, the missionaries themselves. Elizabeth Edwards Bishop, although an extreme example of almost neurotic introspection, never accepted the assurance of grace one might expect from a converting experience. "This carnal mind," she wrote, "attends me in every action of my life." As an applicant for the second company, the then Miss Edwards wrote the Prudential Committee of the American Board of her "desire that the Kingdom of Christ may be built . . . among the heathen." As a bride facing a new life, the young woman worried that she did not care for the "heathen" as she should -- that she lacked the necessary love and compassion to serve the Hawaiians. Mrs. Bishop represents the uncertainty of salvation and worthiness characteristic of many adherents of the Reformed tradition, an uncertainty which by the Second Great Awakening was found more often among women than men. Nevertheless, she did her duty as well as any of the other female assistant missionaries and was well thought of by her colleagues.[2]

The Reverend Charles Stewart represents the more confident aspect of Calvinism, and a more typically male response. Stewart's conversion probably occurred at Litchfield, Connecticut, a center of revivalism, where he read law with Judge Tapping Reeve. The experience changed his life. The young lawyer became a minister and, eventually, accepted the call to mission.

Initially, Stewart had resisted any thoughts of a missionary cause with the excuse that nothing in his life had prepared him for the probable hardship and deprivation of such a life. But friends and teachers continued to encourage him in this direction, especially the Reverend Doctor Ashbel Green, president of the College of New Jersey (later Princeton). Stewart's "experiences upon this point were painful and conflicting for a length of time, but culminated in a

perfect willingness and full resolution to give up and
forsake all and go even into the uttermost parts of the
earth, if it should appear to be the will of
Providence."[3] Missionary enterprise became part of his
duty as a Christian minister.

"To me, the duty involved in Christian Missions to
the heathen, is clear as the sun at noon-day." Stewart
wrote, "to deny it is . . . at once to oppose the whole
spirit and genius of our faith - as well as expressly to
reject the authority of the scriptures. Unto the
Gentiles the Gospel of Jesus must be preached. On whom,
then, does the obligation of this necessity fall?"
Reluctantly, Stewart concluded that the duty fell "on
those ministers of the cross . . . who can devote
themselves to the work, without neglecting or forsaking
a prior and superior duty, incompatible with the
undertaking; and who are not disqualified by physical or
other causes . . . . Of this number, after a careful,
and, . . . at the time unwelcome examination, I proved
myself, to my own conscience, to be one. And what
reason could I plead, why an exception should be granted
to me?"[4]

Stewart tried to find a way of declining the call,
but was unable to do so. Finally, he capitulated, just
as he had eventually accepted the call to repent and the
call to ministry. "This surrender [to mission] was not
made, I admit, without a struggle - not the struggle of
a day - nor of an hour - but of months; and a struggle
of agony too," However, after accepting his fate,
Stewart knew an inner peace.[5]

Once the decision was made, Stewart did not look
back. He was ready to welcome the rude missionary's hut

if by doing so he could most "fully achieve these great ends of existence." The fact that it had taken him so long to acquiesce in God's will, gave Stewart increased confidence that he was pursuing the right cause. "Whatever I myself . . . may suffer, I am fully persuaded, that I have done right . . . . We are not on a warfare at our own charge . . . . We have engaged in this enterprise, not from a sudden impulse of unenlightened enthusiasm, but from a long process of reasoning."[6]

III

The interpretation of the Great Commission in terms of the early years of the Sandwich Islands Mission was both an individual and a collective matter. Theology, revivalism, and the requisite institutions provided a community response to the directive. But the individual stood alone before God, both in his or her theologically acceptable conversion experience and in the acquiescence to the missionary call. Whether the vocation was a truly selfless act, however, the individual could not know. Indeed, even the receipt of grace could be counterfeit.

Personal uncertainty and theological assurance existed in juxtaposition. Not being sure of personal grace, how could the missionaries judge the apparent conversion of the unbeliever? Embarking on a call with little true preparation, what would happen when reality intersected with faith? Perhaps most important, does the Great Commission provide an adequate explanation for such an extensive enterprise?

An historian does not judge matters of faith. He or she describes, analyses and concludes. The historian judges the evidence of what is said and done. But the reader is not passive in the process. It is the reader, after all, who judges the historian. Out of this exchange, it is hoped that both parties gain further insight and understanding of a powerful force in nineteenth century world history.

This study examines four aspects of the Sandwich Islands Mission during its early years in terms of the first twenty-seven individuals to arrive in the field. The first aspect is the Calvinist theology which bound the missionaries together. Second is the application of that theology, both in terms of Puritan missionary efforts among the American Indians, and personal conversions. Third is the founding of the American Board, its development as the institution of missionary activity in New England and the expectations of the cause of missions. Finally, there is an overlapping with previous points as we examine the individual missionaries, their motivations, hopes and experiences.

ACCEPTANCE OF THE GREAT COMMISSION - ENDNOTES

1. For general accounts of missionary activity in
    Hawai'i, see Harold W. Bradley, The American
    Frontier in Hawaii (1942; reprint, Gloucester MA:
    Peter Smith, 1968); Gavan Daws, Shoal of Time
    (Honolulu HI: University of Hawaii Press, 1982);
    Ralph S. Kuykendall, The Hawaiian Kingdom (Honolulu
    HI: University of Hawaii Press, 1978), vol. I.
    Apologists for the cause of missions include Samuel
    C. Bartlett, Historical Sketch of the Missions of
    the American Board in the Sandwich Islands,
    Micronesia and Marquesas (1876; reprint, New York:
    Arno Press, 1972); Oliver W. Elsbree, The Rise of
    the Missionary Spirit in America (1928; reprint,
    Philadelphia: Porcupine Press, 1980); Joseph Tracy,
    "History of the American Board of Commissioners for
    Foreign Missions" in History of American Missions
    to the Heathen from their Commencement to the
    Present Time (Worcester MA: Spooner & Howland,
    1840). For a focus on the political and economic
    motivations of missionaries, see Aarne A. Koskinen,
    Missionary Influence as a Political Factor in the
    Pacific Islands (Helsinki: 1953); Clifton J.
    Phillips, Protestant America and the Pagan World
    (Boston: Harvard East Asian Monographs, 1969)..
    Institutional motivations for the entire missionary
    enterprise are discussed by John A. Andrew,
    Rebuilding the Christian Commonwealth (Lexington
    KY: The University Press of Kentucky, 1976). Hiram
    Bingham's personal, non-religious motivations for
    mission are discussed by Char Miller, Fathers and
    Sons (Philadelphia: Temple University Press, 1982),
    chapter 1.

2. Elizabeth Edwards Bishop, April 4, 1822, January
    22, 1823, Journal, Journal Collection (hereinafter
    referred to as JC), Mission Children's Society
    Library, Honolulu HI (hereinafter referred to as
    HMCSL). Elizabeth Edwards, Letters of Candidacy;
    Elizabeth Edwards to the Prudential Committee,
    November 8, 1822; Elizabeth Edwards Bishop to Mrs.
    G. Thomas, December 16, 1822, Missionary Letters
    (hereinafter referred to as ML), HMCSL.

3. Charles Stewart, Letters of Candidacy; Charles
    Stewart to the Prudential Committee, November 1,
    1821, ML, HMCSL.

4. Charles Stewart, <u>Journal of a Residence in the Sandwich Islands 1823-1825</u> (1830; reprint, Honolulu HI: University of Hawaii Press, 1970), p. 44.

5. Ibid., p. 45.

6. Ibid., pp. 42-43.

CHAPTER II

GOD'S SOVEREIGNTY: A THEOLOGICAL PROBLEM

> "For whom he did foreknow, he also did
> predestinate to be conformed to the image of
> his Son, that he might be the firstborn among
> many brethren. Moreover whom he did
> predestinate, them he also called: and whom he
> called, them he also glorified." (Romans
> 8:29-30)

The foundation of the New England missionary
enterprise rests upon the Calvinist theology of the
Reformed tradition. This intellectual system with its
shifting definition of who was saved and who was not
determined the missionaries' perception of themselves
and their potential converts as they struggled to
fulfill God's law. It shaped their view concerning the
essential "humanity" of the unbeliever; the relationship
of "true religion" to culture, and the interaction of
church and state. Perhaps most of all, Calvinist
theology left even those individuals who had abandoned
all else to do what they perceived as God's will in a
perpetual state of uncertainty regarding their personal
salvation.

In the early nineteenth century the average New
Englander with even the slightest interest in religion
came into contact with the entire spectrum of Calvinist
thought, if not from a direct reading of the theological
volumes, then through the popular piety espoused by such
publications as the **Panoplist** and the **Christian
Advocate**. These advocated both the delineation of
obscure theological points and the necessity of action

upon them. Popular theology, then, had a slight element of shifting sands as it fluctuated from Cotton Mather to Samuel Hopkins or Lyman Beecher, and continued the fight against the ever-growing appeal of arminianism.[1] The central question of salvation was constant, but the answer contained variable elements.

II

The development of Calvinist theology revolved around questions of who was saved and what the individual must do to be saved. To Calvinists, these questions shaped the relationship of man and God, man and man, man and his environment. They were difficult questions, because ultimately the gift of salvation rested with God, and since this was so, man had no control over his destiny. This was a situation modern man could not accept. Consequently, Calvinist theology tried to balance the opposing concepts of the sovereignty of God and the powerlessness of men; the reasonable mercy of God and the participation of men in their own salvation.

There were several issues: whether works were the cause or result of salvation; whether salvation was experiential, leaving all power with God, or contractual, giving man varying amounts of control over his destiny; the role of the state in salvation, and the arrival of God's Kingdom. The answer to these issues and their evolution over time laid the foundation not only for the message proclaimed by the missionaries to the Sandwich Islanders, but also their method of proclamation.

The founder of the Reform tradition was John Calvin whose Institutes of the Christian Religion (1536) synthesized Protestant thought up to that time, and established a systematic theology governing both secular and spiritual concerns. This system as implemented at Geneva provided a tangible example of a Christian society.

The Reform tradition had several basic features. The central precept was that of God's total and complete sovereignty. This brought about the logical conclusion of man's total depravity and the doctrine of double predestination, that is, that some were elected to salvation and others to damnation. This, of course, raised the problem of identifying those in the former category, designated by the term Elect. Given the situation, there was extreme concern for God's law as revealed in the Bible. It was paramount that the visible church be "reformed" to that state described in scripture.

John Calvin's concept of predestination was at once harsher and gentler than later Puritan interpretations. According to that concept, regeneration was not a sudden and cataclysmic experience, but a gradual process of growth in grace begun at baptism and continuing throughout the individual's life. Those who experienced this growth in faith under the guidance of the church and its ministers, and who participated in the sacraments and lived an upright life could count themselves among the Elect. Calvin encouraged all those within the church to believe in their election. They had merely to wait upon God's pleasure.

The other side of this doctrine was the insecurity the individual must feel regarding his salvation. One lived as though he or she were saved, but the individual could never be sure of entering an elected state. Since man was passive in the reception of grace, there was nothing the individual could do to improve his or her chances. Although Calvin taught that grace began at baptism, one could never be confident of one's status before God.

Calvin also espoused a covenant theology demonstrating that predestination was not as harsh as it first appeared. God had established a Covenant of Grace with the seed of Abraham which was enacted via faith and, therefore, a personal encounter between God and his creature. The encounter was always at God's initiative, but by the Covenant of Redemption God contracted with his Son, Jesus, for the salvation of mankind. Although passive until the reception of grace which brought faith, the individual was then expected through a process of preparation, dedication and gratitude to obey God's Law. The Reformed tradition was, therefore, an active one.

The insecurity of election could not easily be borne, particularly in areas where the Reformed were a distinct minority. English Puritans, in their efforts to distinguish their "purity" and uniqueness, became obsessed with the idea that neither evangelical religion nor baptism was sufficient. Rather, there must be a tangible transition from an unregenerate state of nature to a spiritual state of grace before a candidate received admission to the sacraments. Evidence of this transition became an initiation rite into the Puritan sect that both lessened the opportunities for those without true conversion obtaining entrance and further separated Puritans from their unregenerate Anglican brethren.

Conversion became a difficult process. The individual no longer remained passive in the reception of grace, but took an active part in a preparation process, thereby increasing his or her chances of election. God had now bound Himself by a covenant that allowed people to use their natural gifts in order to accept God's offer of an agreement and apply the means of grace such as good works and self-discipline. These brought faith and eventual justification. Thus, faith became the active element in claiming God's mercy. Such a development provided the converted with the assurance of salvation, but it also chipped away at the absolute sovereignty of God.

This change in the criteria of conversion was crucial to the development of sixteenth century English Puritanism as a church community. Those who testified to their Elect status bound themselves to a covenant between themselves and God as a body of Visible Saints. No longer would the church be open to all as a means of grace; it was now a disciplined community. Thus, it is clear that the Law not only improved the individual's spiritual state, but it also provided the standard to which the world must conform. Calvin's politics had been based on a recognition of political realities and the demand that these must serve religious purposes. Calvin recognized a permanent estrangement of human beings and God which manifested itself in the need for external controls over people. The Fall had created a creature who always struggled to dominate, and therefore, sometimes required repression to subdue. Yet, God demanded voluntary obedience. The need, then, was for church and state to work together in a Christian commonwealth, founded on the consent of conscientious citizens. This brought coercion and conscience together, and recognized that social control was increased if people have consented to it.

Despite the unity of commonwealth, church and state remained separate. They intersected at the point where laymen served in the government. The church member brought the church's moral tone into government as well as a sense of religious responsibility represented in the enactment of various civil laws.

Thus, civil government could contribute to grace. A citizen might first obey a law from external pressure, but after receiving grace, the law was written on his heart and coercion was no longer needed. This was the beginning of a true Christian commonwealth. Calvin's interpretation took religious reform from an individual to a community experience. This idea could be further extended, as it was in New England, to bind the entire society into external conformity with God's Law.

While the conversion itself remained a private affair between God and the applicant, the ministerial office provided the crucial link between God and man. It was the minister who bore the witness to God's truth to all who would listen, as if they would be saved. The minister also imparted moral authority which greatly influenced the secular government through the presence of church members in magisterial offices.

Within New England society, everyone walked a close line. To do otherwise was to court disaster from both God and man. Despite the fact that each individual must meet God alone in spiritual life, he or she dealt with

God as a member of the community in secular life. It was crucial that God should smile upon the colony, and therefore that all its citizens must adhereto the Law. Training in communal identity began during early childhood, and made the concepts of self and community inseparable. Initially, this training was through physical coercion and humiliation. Cotton Mather (1663-1728), however, popularized a method called "anxiety" which served to ensure not only external conformity, but the development of a hyperactive conscience and moral autonomy leading the individual to push for ever higher standards and achievements.

Social training became increasingly important during late seventeenth century New England. Members of the new generation were not coming forward for church membership, because they were unable or unwilling to submit to the conversion experience. Since church membership was a pre-requisite for political participation, leading families were threatened with the loss of political power. In order to resolve this crisis, Mather and other theologians turned to Genesis 17:7 to demonstrate that the covenant had been made by God with Abraham and his posterity.[2] Puritan children belonged to the covenant through baptism and even if they showed no signs of grace, they probably were saved. Thus, baptism became the only prerequisite for church and state participation. The unregenerate baptized could indicate their intellectual assent to the covenant allowing them to baptize their children and to vote on secular issues.

This Half-Way Covenant was a temporary compromise at best. It encouraged a legalism and a blurring of works and grace which did nothing to halt the process of declension. Without a converting experience, religion became lifeless and unappealing.

III

The Great Awakening (1740-1742) was a natural consequence of declension. There had been a few preceding revivals, primarily in Solomon Stoddard's Northamption, but the problem of declension had remained unsolved.[3] After succeeding to Stoddard's parish, Jonathan Edwards led a revival from 1734 to 1736 which spread throughout the immediate area. Edwards was not totally sure of the cause; he had preached for some years without visible effect. Other forces had touched people's hearts. For example, Edwards reported an incident at Puscommuck, a village near Northampton.

> In the April following, anno 1734, there happened a <u>sudden and awful death of a young man</u> in the bloom of his youth; who being violently seized with <u>pleurisy</u>, and taken immediately very <u>delirious</u>, died in about <u>two days</u>; which (together with what was preached publically on that occasion) <u>much affected</u> many young people. This was followed with another death of a young married woman, who had been considerably <u>exercised</u> in mind, about the salvation of her soul, before she was ill, and was in great <u>distress</u>, in the beginning of her illness; but seemed to have <u>satisfying evidences</u> of God's proving <u>mercy</u> to her, before her death; so that she died very full of <u>comfort</u>, in a most earnest and moving manner <u>warning</u>, and counselling others. This seemed to <u>contribute</u> to render solemn the spirits of many young persons; and there began evidently to appear more of a <u>religious concern</u> on people's minds.[4]

These Northampton revivals proved that God still worked with men and prepared the way for a general awakening; however, there was no fiery renewal until

George Whitefield traveled through New England in 1740. Whitefield's arrival coincided with a diphtheria epidemic, the economic recession brought about by the War of Jenkins' Ear in the West Indies (1739), and the general social changes brought about by growing mobility on the frontier and the new emphasis on personal rather than landed wealth. These factors had begun a crisis which the revival would relieve.

Whitefield was an immediate sensation. Whitefield's sermons were simple; his Calvinism was adaptable. Whitefield's impression of New England was that it would have a successful revival of the spirit, because "[the clergy] are more simple in their worship, less corrupt in their principles, and consequently more easily brought over to the form of sound words, into which so many of their pious ancestors were delivered."[5]

As a result of the efforts of Whitefield and other itinerant preachers, there was a revival of experiential piety, and conversion returned to its previous central position. Evangelists depicted the natural state of the unconverted as one of sleepiness. Despite regular church attendance, the unregenerate suffered from pride and the assumption that their works were acceptable to God. Thus, the first step was conviction, the sinner's realization of his sinfulness and inability before finally submitting to God's judgment. The sinner then received grace, and the reliance on Christ which changed his relationship to God and to his neighbors. Conviction occurred as a response to the revival or a sermon. Conversion occurred via Scripture which opened one's eyes to God's truth. The process was so cataclysmic and the new regenerate so aware of his former sinful state that he could only identify those who opposed the revival as being under Satan's power.

Jonathan Edwards was the systematic theologian who not only developed the methodology of revivals and the criteria for judging conversions, but also laid the foundation of the evangelical theology which would prevail until the mid-nineteenth century. A committed Calvinist who looked to the ancestral roots, Edwards was influenced also by the Enlightenment and its use of reason, logic and sensation.

Edwards was always a devout young man with an interest in science, but as a Yale graduate at the age of seventeen, Edwards underwent a conversion which brought his knowledge of science, love of nature and reverent affection for God into a permanent and lasting union. His heart was touched after reading I Timothy 1:17,[6] and soon after young Jonathan

> walked abroad alone . . . for contemplation. And as I was walking there and looking up on the sky and clouds, there came to my mind so sweet a sense of the glorious majesty and grace of God, that I know not how to express. I seemed to see them both in a sweet conjunction; majesty and meekness joined together . . . After this my sense of divine things gradually increased, and became more and more lively, and had more of that inward sweetness. The appearance of every thing was altered; there seemed to be . . . a calm, sweet cast or appearance of divine glory, in almost every thing. God's excellency, his wisdom, his purity and love, seemed to appear in every thing; in the sun, moon and stars; in the clouds, and blue sky; in the grass, flowers, trees; in the water and all nature.[7]

The wonder of the experience never left Edwards and is evident in all his work. Edwards was not simply a mystic who had only to seek union with God. Instead Edwards believed that such a union of God and his creature was an ongoing process, because the creature could never achieve the infinite perfection necessary to make that union complete. Thus, conversion was not a goal to be attained, but a state to be acted upon.

As Edwards surveyed the dismal state of New England piety, he perceived that Calvin's original concepts of covenant and divine sovereignty had been denigrated to a point of subjectivism which equated faith with salvation, with the result that man assumed the central position in religion. This comforting and ostensibly logical approach destroyed vital religion, because it pretended that the choice rested with man, not God.

Edwards' approach of theological objectivism looked to God as the source of religion and affirmed divine primacy in metaphysics, moralism and spirituality. The flaw in the original Puritan concept was that of a fluctuation in the quality of faith. It seemed that sometimes God bestowed the necessary emotional component of faith and sometimes He did not, with the resulting development of legalism. The Edwardsean concept corrected this flaw by the addition of reason. Edwards was especially influenced in this regard by John Locke's <u>An Essay Concerning Human Understanding</u> which stated that people acquired reason and knowledge from sensate experiences. The mind received these sense impressions and the perception of ideas that were a part of these impressions. From this Lockean thesis Edwards derived two key concepts: first, that a man becomes what he willfully perceives himself to be; second, that since perceptions derive from the senses, man's self-perception depends on his sense of the heart. This approach remedied the problem of fluctuating faith, because the individual could now perceive whatever state of faith he wished to attain.

In order to generate the required sensations, Edwards utilized Christian speech by using the words most apt to create the sensations and the ideas attached to them within the hearts of his listeners. Such a preaching style touched the passive hearts and minds of sinners, calling them into action and faith. Edwards emphasized God's glory and man's self-interest in his efforts to swell the ranks of God's Kingdom on earth.

Edwards joined his grandfather, Solomon Stoddard, in the parish of Northampton in 1727, and remained there after Stoddard's death. It was a fortuitous call, because the Northampton congregation was both accustomed to theological innovation and experienced in the phenomenon of religious revival. In addition, "Pope" Stoddard had established Northampton as the leading congregation in the Connecticut River Valley. Edwards' first four years there were uneventful. The young minister established a modest reputation for his development of a rational Calvinism, but his parishioners did not exhibit any sort of religious fervor. In 1734, Edwards began a series of sermons directed against Arminianism.

The sermon entitled Justification by Faith Alone clearly represented the Edwardsean response to the

Arminian doctrine of free will. "It is in this doctrine
that the most essential difference lies between the
covenant of grace and the first covenant." Arminianism
"supposes that we are justified by our works . . . . It
is not gospel at all; it is law: it is no covenant of
grace, but of works: it is not an evangelical, but a
legal doctrine."[8]

Edwards found even the suggestion of reliance on
works to be preposterous. "Will it not betray a
foolish, exalting opinion of ourselves, and a mean one
of God," he wrote, "to have a thought of offering any
thing of ours, to recommend us to the favor of being
brought from wallowing, like filthy swine, in the mire
of our sins, and from the enmity and misery of devils in
the lowest hell, to the state of God's dear children."
Rather, "we should believe in the general according to
the clear and abundant revelations of God's word that it
is none of our own excellency, virtue or righteousness,
that is the ground of our being received from a state of
condemnation into a state of acceptance in God's sight,
but only Jesus Christ, and his righteousness and
worthiness, received by faith."[9]

These themes of sovereignty of God, dependency
of man and the need for Christ's justification touched
people, and Edwards was gratified by the outpouring of
the Holy Spirit in Northampton during the years 1734 to
1736. Having unleashed the revival, Edwards immediately
attempted to record and guide it. In 1737, he published
Narrative of the Surprising Work of God in the
Conversion of Many Hundred Souls in Northampton and
Neighboring Towns and Villages, a work that not only
brought Edwards notoriety, but also established

guidelines for discerning those who had been genuinely
affected by the Spirit.

Edwards returned to John Calvin's assertion that
the key to religion was the recognition of God's
sovereignty, His total moral perfection and His right to
damn or save as He pleased; these were the
manifestations of God's glory. As Edwards exalted God's
glory, he deprecated man; as he demonstrated God's
saving power, he revealed God's graciousness, and
thereby joined divine judgment with divine benevolence.
These ideas became public at nearby Enfield, where
Edwards preached <u>Sinners in the Hands of an Angry God</u>.
The sermon vividly depicted man's helplessness as
Edwards demonstrated the emptiness of the purely
rational approach and the necessity of a passionate
appeal to the senses.

Edwards' personal commitment to divine authority
made him aware of the need to uphold that authority at
the expense of personal gain. During the Northampton
revival, parishioners told Edwards of their new sense of
God's justice and their willingness to be damned because
of their unworthiness. This willingness to bear all for
God's glory gave regenerates energy to oppose all who
questioned their regenerate state, and to save those who
remained unconverted. Edwardseans believed that any
opponent of the reviving work of the Spirit was of the
devil and were apt to perceive the unregenerate as
victims of spiritual pride. "Those that are themselves
cold and dead," Edwards wrote, "and especially such as
never had any experience of the power of Godliness on
their own hearts, are ready to entertain such thoughts
of the best Christians; which arises from a secret

enmity against vital and fervent piety."[10]

Edwards' first major theological work was A Treatise Concerning Religious Affections (1746), his first printed denouncement of contractual theology. The treatise found religion to rest in the affections, primarily love, and that these affections were manifest in Christian practice. Edwards believed that "although to true religion there must indeed be something else besides affections; yet true religion consists so much in the affections, that there can be no true religion without them." He recognized also that "there are false affections, and there are true. A man's having such affection does not prove that he has any true religion; but if he has no affection, it proves he has no true religion."[11]

This affection, or love, of God "makes a man have desires of the honor of God, and desire to please him . . . love to God causes a man to delight in the thoughts of God, and to delight in the presence of God, and to desire conformity with God, and the enjoyment of God." Such affection led to a spiritual understanding of God's perfection and works. The evidence of such affection and understanding was its practical exercise to conquer the corruption of men and lead them into holiness. "Christian practice . . . is the chief of all the evidence of a saving sincerity in religion . . . much to be preferred to the method of the first convictions, enlightenings, and comforts in conversion, or any immanent discoveries or exercises of grace whatsoever, that begin and end in contemplation." Religious sincerity was to place God first in one's life; godliness was to do His will. Salvation imparted the responsibility for action.[12]   The implications of this treatise would achieve fruition in the voluntary societies of the early nineteenth century.

As the revivals continued, conversion seemed within the reach of all and a reassertion of a church of Visible Saints did not seem unreasonable.   In 1747, Edwards closed communion to all but Visible Saints, thereby depriving many members of the Sacrament.   This decision was one of a series of differences between Edwards and his flock, and the congregation removed him. In 1750, Edwards accepted the call from a missionary congregation at Stockbridge.

There Edwards continued his battle against Arminianism.   The treatises written at Stockbridge, however, differ from Edwards' previous efforts both in their theological profundity and future impact, exerting the greater influence on the future of American evangelism.   A Careful and Strict Enquiry into the modern prevailing Notions of that Freedom of Will, Which is supposed to be essential to Moral Agency, Value and Vice, Reward and Punishment, Praise and Blame (1754) continued the attack on Arminianism begun in Religious Affections.   Edwards concluded that, at best, freedom was the opportunity to exercise the predetermined will of God without external coercion. The   treatise   also discussed sin and defined it less as wrongdoing than a failure to cleave to God's glory for its own sake.   Sin could never be alleviated by good deeds, because it was an infinite offense made against an infinite Being.

Edwards' ideas on sin were further explored in The Great Christian Doctrine of Original Sin Defended (1758) in which he grappled with the problem of whether

God's sovereignty extended to the cause of sin. Edwards concluded that God was not the source of evil. The reason for man's depravity lay with Adam's fall, because with this act man lost his initial impulse toward benevolence and replaced it with self-love. Thus, the natural unregenerate man was motivated by his own desire for happiness. The difference salvation brought was the idea that happiness lay in loving God's happiness and glory as well as one's own so that one would pursue God's will which has become one with the individual's own self-interest.

As Edwards wrote on original sin, he was also preparing a treatise On the Nature of True Virtue (1765). Published posthumously, this work and its companion, Dissertation Concerning the End for which God Created the World, were not only the culmination of Edwards' thought, but also the foundation for the continuance of revivalism in the Second Great Awakening. Consistent with his points on free will, Edwards discussed the limited abilities of the natural man. Through reason man was instructed in his duty to obey God and fulfill moral responsibilities. He intellectually appreciated divine beauty and virtue, and understood his vulnerable state before a just God. These reasonable conclusions were worthless in terms of man's salvation, but they were a means of preparation for reasonable men. (Those unregenerate who lack in intellectual powers must have more graphic representations of the danger of their state.) Natural man, then, lived in a world of awareness and self-interest, but the sin of self-love had separated him from God and true virtue.

Regeneration brought man to a state of true virtue, i.e., a state of benevolence to Being in general. Edwards shifted divine identity from the concept of God to that of "Being in general," because the latter more clearly demonstrated the basis of piety, love to both God and man. Grace implanted such benevolent affection in the believer's heart that he now perceived the awesome beauty of divine virtue. Man now partook of God's moral beauty, working to maintain this new unity with the divine will by acting upon it. Thus, virtue not only brought man to a mystical perception of God's profound beauty, but also to a state of active work in doing God's will. This became the impetus of worldly work in terms of evangelism, abolition, temperance and other reform societies. These became not only the fruits of salvation, but also proof of one's union with God.

The phenomenon of Jonathan Edwards is crucial to our understanding of the future development of both Calvinism and its fruits. Edwards laid the Puritan synthesis to rest. That synthesis had always been a strained one as Puritans tried to walk between the spiritual and rational elements of their understanding. Changing American conditions increased the strain as the spiritual element was de-emphasized and a less pious society looked for the very legalism which had driven their founders out of the Church of England. Edwards brought together Calvinist and Enlightenment thought to produce a synthesis of both traditions, and used this new approach to touch the sensations of the unregenerate.

The concepts which Edwards labored to establish

did not come to fruition until his Stockbridge years. Then the divergent wings came together as Edwards logically and rationally presented the role of natural man in God's universe. Both intellectual and spiritual understanding were a part of the divine plan, but alone neither could conceive of that joyous union of God and the Elect, the cataclysm in which their wills became one. Out of this mystical event men would build God's Kingdom on earth. Unfortunately, such insight came to few, and Edwards' disciples, unable to truly understand his systematic theology, inadvertently altered it as they put it into practical use.

IV

Edwards' efforts to establish a new theological paradigm were continued by his students, Samuel Hopkins and Joseph Bellamy.[13] These men and their adherents wore several labels; Edwardseans, consistent Calvinists, the New Divinity. Hopkins developed the concept of "disinterested benevolence" while Bellamy wrote of "evangelical humiliation," yet their goals were the same. Both men attempted to build a complete and consistent system of practical, evangelical Calvinism around the issues of nature, the need for spiritual rebirth, the authenticity of mass conversions, the role of means in the process of regeneration, and the coming millennium. Despite the desire of the New Divinity to encourage further revival, intense metaphysical debates coupled with secular events frustrated this aspiration until spiritual and secular concerns reunited about 1790.

The New Divinity men comprised about five percent of New England's clergy. Their theological system was most appealing to young men of obscure social background, often from frontier areas where conversion experience counted for more than social standing. New Divinity theologians usually held Yale degrees, but parish ministers were typically trained at a "School for Prophets." Bellamy's school was especially popular. These schools served to transmit the lifestyle and professional values of the Edwardseans. New Divinity ministers were less interested in pastoral duties or their own personal comforts than in the need for systematic theology and preparation for the millennium.

New Divinity theology kept the kingpin of divine sovereignty and the necessity of God's punishment of sin in order to uphold moral order, but these theologians also believed in general atonement which meant that more souls would be saved than lost. They worried that people would misinterpret the Edwardsean concept of self-interest; and that rather than equating God's will with their own, they would pursue their own personal interests without considering God's plan. This potential problem was countered with Hopkins' concept of disinterested benevolence.

Samuel Hopkins, whose theological approach would have a major impact on early nineteenth century missionary activity, did not undergo a true converting experience prior to his arrival at Yale. Here fellow students David Brainerd and Gilbert Tennent, both active in the Great Awakening, discussed the necessity of the converting experience with a young, insecure Hopkins, already deeply impressed by Whitefield's preaching. One evening while at private devotions, the event took place. "The character of Jesus Christ the Mediator came into view, and appeared such a reality and so glorious and the way of salvation by him so wise, important and desirable, that I was astonished at myself, that I had never seen these things before, which were so plain, pleasing and desirable . . . . I was greatly affected in view of my own depravity, the sinfulness, odiousness and guilt of my character, and tears flowed in great plenty."[14] The remainder of Hopkins' conversion was so gradual that he could never precisely date the event, for from that moment his focus was on Jesus, not salvation. As a result of this experience, Hopkins' concept of disinterested benevolence required that the man who is truly saved be unconcerned about salvation.

After graduation, Hopkins spent two years with Edwards before accepting a call to Housatonic (later Great Barrington) in 1743. Hopkins remained there with a sense of self-denial which further influenced his concept of disinterested benevolence. The young minister was very close to Edwards, editing the great man's papers after his death, and responsible for Edwards' posthumous publications. Yet despite this close association, Hopkins deviated from the spirit of Edwards.

Hopkins' first major work, An Inquiry into Promise of the Gospel (1756), described the election process. Hopkins differed with Edwards on the idea of original sin. He did not accept the premise that all men participated in Adam's fall, rather, Hopkins believed that Adam alone was responsible for his own sin, and that future generations were responsible only to the extent they approved Adam's choice. Those generations demonstrated their approval by participating in sin by their own choice. Man had the choice of repentance and should be exhorted to repent, but he would not have success until he had a change of heart.

The sinner, then, was wicked and under immediate obligation to repent, but he could not do this without regeneration, a passive acceptance of grace. Regeneration could be hoped for only through knowledge, repentance, and God's mercy; it provided the new heart that made conversion possible. The individual had no awareness of this transition until he realized a change in his thoughts and acts, a turning to God and Scripture. "There must . . . be a distinction kept up between regeneration which is the work of God in giving a new heart, and in which men are perfectly passive, and active conversion, in which men, being regenerated, turn from sin to God in the exercise of repentance towards God and faith towards our Lord Jesus Christ, and in consequence of which they are pardoned and received to favor and a title to eternal life."[15] Thus, passivity in the reception of grace remained, but predestination was undermined; salvation was offered to all who seriously desired it. It must, therefore, be presented to all, so that truth could be brought out and the unconverted discern divine things. The Elect would use these means for repentance, however, the unregenerate would not be moved, with two possible results. The sinner might simply reject the Gospel out of hand, or he might try to repent, not for the love of God, but to save himself. Without real desire for change, however, the sinner would inevitably fail. This explained those people whose hearts were touched at every revival. In either

case, those sinners who chose to remain unregenerate
were more despised by God than those in a state of
ignorance.

Hopkins' later ideas were largely a reaction
against Edwards' concepts of "true virtue" and "Being in
general." Hopkins' misgivings in this regard first
occurred in 1765 but his conclusions were not developed
until the publication of <u>An Inquiry into the Nature of
True Holiness</u> (1773). Edwardsean theology, the years at
Housatonic, and the experience of serving the First
Congregational Church of Newport, Rhode Island, all
influenced Hopkinsian theology. In urban, prosperous
Newport Hopkins was confronted with "good" people who
profited from the misery of the slave trade and reacted
strongly against the possibility that this might be a
prototype for America's future. Hopkins found that
Calvinist social values did not work in a changing
America where communal values were rapidly evolving
toward acquisitive, egocentric norms. Edwards' works
were too abstract to deal with these worldly problems.
Rather than spurring people to salvation and social
action, they led to passive contemplation and mystic
otherworldliness.

By holiness, Hopkins meant the opposite of
self-love. To him, self-love was the sin which blinded
the heart to moral excellence and was responsible for
the world's impiety. Holiness, then, was universal,
disinterested benevolence. While Edwards described
benevolence as the total of God's attributes, Hopkins
equated benevolence with God. So, to practice
benevolence was to act in accordance with God's nature
and will. Benevolence required that one love others as

much as the self; only then could the individual make necessary sacrifices for the greater good.

Hopkins denied the existence of natural virtue, because it was a concept borrowed from rational philosophy that was both ethically and spiritually dangerous in its reliance on self-love. Hopkins believed people were dominated by either self-interest or virtue. If one chose to love God because he realized it was in his self-interest not to be damned, then he did not in fact love God but himself. In such a situation the individual was attempting to avoid hell, not serve God. Salvation required that the individual remain unaware of his love for God, and even be willing to be damned in order to serve God's greater glory. Such damnation was not something for the individual to be pleased with, or even desire. It simply implied a willingness to make any sacrifice necessary for the greater good. In short, the individual should be completely indifferent to all that related to the self, even salvation. Such an idea was the opposite of the sensationalism Edwards used.

Sinners reached the state of virtue by means of "disinterested benevolence." By disinterested benevolence the sinner demonstrated his love of God and of his neighbor by losing himself in a cause higher than personal salvation. One worked for the temporal and eternal well-being of others. Thus, disinterested benevolence was more than saving souls. It was the desire to relieve suffering. It must be practiced towards all, including heathens who were spiritually perishing because Christians were failing to practice disinterested benevolence. "In the practice of the greatest self-denial a person does not divest himself of a love of happiness," Hopkins wrote, "but he places his happiness, not in his own private interest but in a good more worthy to be sought, viz., the glory of God, and the prosperity of his church and kingdom. For the sake of this he gives up the former and forgets himself."[16] Disinterested benevolence provided a primary feature of the Second Great Awakening by its call to action. It was a call which complemented the millennial expectations of the evangelicals and gave the penitent a concrete opportunity to do God's work.

Joseph Bellamy also brought a greater sense of pragmatism to Edwards' work. Like Hopkins he was a Yale graduate and student of Edwards. Bellamy served as an itinerant preacher for two years during the Great Awakening, and later established a frontier seminary at Bethlehem, Connecticut. Bellamy was more oriented towards the needs of his audience than Hopkins, and although he largely agreed with Edwards, Bellamy made certain key departures from both Edwards and Hopkins. In True Religion Delineated (1750) Bellamy found that "as to natural capacity, all mankind are capable of a perfect conformity to God's law, which requires us only to love God with all our hearts: and that our inability arises merely from the bad temper of our hearts."[17] This inability was grounds for repentance. Sin itself was voluntary, a decision made in the sinner's heart. Therefore, preachers must realize that sinners can repent and exhort them to do so immediately.

Bellamy made a major departure in his discussion of election and atonement. He believed that election was not due to man's actions, nor to God's capriciousness. God was required to exercise love and act for the welfare of being. God always acted from love and the interests of his creatures rather than from his own sovereignty. So, Christ did not die only for the Elect. If that were so, God could not save other believers. Rather, Christ died for all. Once an individual repented and loved God, he was capable of loving his neighbor. Yet, to love God out of fear of damnation was selfish, and, therefore, did not lead to salvation. Bellamy wrote that regeneration was the result of an "evangelical humiliation" in which the individual became so aware of his sins that he was filled with self-loathing as he appeared before God.

The New Divinity represented a definite departure from its mentor, Jonathan Edwards. Because the New Divinity men did not appreciate the subtleties of Edwards' understanding of virtue, they attempted to remove the sensational component in favor of a discouraging legalist logic which also lessened the harshness of predestination.

While the New Divinity men adjusted Edwardsean theology, however, Americans went on to the sensory experience of war and rumors of war (1756-1783). Such activities usually turn men's minds from religion, but the use of Puritan rhetorical imagery which at various times equated both France and Great Britain with the Anti-Christ kept religious values firmly in mind.

V

Post-revolutionary New England saw the blending of the various strands of Calvinist tradition in the Second Great Awakening (1790-1840). Sensationalism joined with theology, and religion with the virtues of good citizenship as the new republic struggled to find its intellectual footing. Calvin, Edwards, Bellamy, Hopkins and the Puritan forefathers were all offered as serious reading material. The republican ideal of a virtuous citizenry working for the general good seemed compatible with the Hopkinsian aspiration of disinterested benevolence. As the political excitement of revolution diffused into the confusion of the postwar period, New Englanders turned again to religious concerns and soon identified their clerical partners in the struggle for salvation.

The first giant of the new revivalism was Timothy Dwight, a grandson of Jonathan Edwards, who had studied theology with his uncle, Jonathan Edwards the Younger. Dwight served as a chaplain during the American revolution, and became greatly concerned about the moral fiber of the new nation. He believed that there was much in the contemporary situation which presaged the millennium. The revolution had been God's vengeance on Great Britain for her selfishness, and presented a new opportunity for progress, but it had brought also a new skepticism of religion which must be crushed. Dwight believed the new nation must be humble before God since its very existence was due to God's sovereignty, and that such humility would intersect with the political need for virtue.

In 1795, Dwight preached "The True Means of Establishing Public Happiness" in response to the Whiskey Rebellion (1794). In it he asserted that freedom alone was not enough, that men could be free and still be miserable. The true aim in life must not be freedom but happiness which could only occur by way of the virtue that comes from a religious education and public worship.[18] Politics could never be separated from morality and were a function of a moral society. Freedom was the reward which Americans received for their spiritual character and moral virtue. The relationship of religion and the state must be reciprocal and inseparable. Religion provided good citizens and good laws while the state supported both high moral standards and religious education in addition to setting an example through its public officials.

Dwight marked a return to the idea of free agency as God became less autocratic and more republican. God now clearly called man to voluntary obedience, and a contractual faith by which man received grace in exchange for his trust in God. God's foreknowledge was no longer a hindrance to man's free action. In fact, Dwight suggested that such metaphysical subjects as predestination were not fit sermon topics, because they confused listeners. Dwight wanted to simplify religion. In his effort to revive experiential piety, Dwight stressed human activity and the use of means.

The two natural means to salvation were religious education and public worship, the very institutions Dwight recommended to a virtuous citizenry. These means would train the will in the proper direction. When the educator was successful in his persuasion, it was because the Spirit enlivened educator's preaching and restored the souls, yet the institution provided the Spirit with the opportunity to touch men's hearts. Saving grace was the regular effect of a virtuous environment, and God's sovereignty was exercised as He placed man in an environment suitable or unsuitable for the growth of piety and eventual salvation. However, though God might place man in a conducive environment, man still had power to resist the Spirit. Man's submission to God came from the fear and love he might feel for a stern parent. Above all, man's submission was voluntary.

Dwight made two major departures from the New Divinity. First, he found the idea that a man must be willing to be damned if he would be saved abhorrent and asserted that God's glory rested in man's happiness. Consequently, Christians were unable to wish themselves damned even for God's glory. Dwight further stressed the importance of fruits over the inward state of piety, and even declared that one could resist the Spirit and still do His work. Dwight conceded the importance of the inward state, but not its absolute requirement. Such an attitude would encourage both the regenerate and those aspiring to that state to participate in voluntary societies.

Dwight never fully relinquished the New Divinity but his modifications gave way to a new approach which blossomed in the 1820s and 1830s under the leadership of two of his students, Lyman Beecher and Nathaniel Taylor. A doer with little interest in pure theology, Beecher would stretch Dwight as far as possible before his partnership with Taylor. The joint efforts of Beecher and Taylor gave birth to the New Haven Theology and the use of "new measures." Taylor took Dwight's alterations to their natural conclusion that if man was free, God must be limited. Such a philosophy was necessary for maximum results at a revival, and was, in part, responsible for keeping the revival fires lit through the 1840s.

Dwight is often given credit for igniting the Second Great Awakening by a three year series of sermons, Theology Explained and Defended, presented at Yale (1799-1802). This credit is in error, since Dwight's first showers of 1802 occurred fully three years after the first great wave of revivals while his students at this time were too young to hold leadership positions in the movement. The fact that several of the early revival leaders had studied with Bellamy and Edwards the Younger demonstrates that the New Divinity remained a strong force in the early nineteenth century.

Dwight's Theology, however, served to prove that orthodoxy was man's most useful system in providing happiness. Dwight used these sermons as a vehicle for harmonizing Calvinism with the new American values. Within this system revelation superseded regeneration as the source of truth. Faith in doctrine was not enough; one must also be concerned with God's law.[19]

Dwight found divine law the source of perfect happiness. As people followed that law, they became praiseworthy and God rewarded them with happiness. The purpose of divine law was God's glory and the law could be enacted only by intelligent beings. The first law was to love God which included goodwill and benevolence to all God's designs and gratitude for his kindness; violation of this law was the source of all sin.

> We unite with God, and the virtuous universe in voluntarily promoting that supreme good, which by his own perfections, and their instrumentality, he has begun to accomplish.
> This work is literally divine . . .
> an immense and eternal kingdom of virtue

> and happiness: all that wisdom can
> approve or virtue desire . . . . To
> choose it, is to exhibit the best of all
> characters. It is to choose what God
> himself chooses; to act, as he acts; and
> to be <u>fellow workers together with him</u>
> in the glorious edifice of eternal
> good.[20]

All had a part in God's work, and all must actively follow the two commandments of moral law, i.e., the love of God and one's neighbor. The disposition of this law was "<u>disinterested love</u>, or <u>the Spirit of doing good</u>."[21]

Dwight's emphasis on the laws to love God and one's neighbor demonstrate that despite his quarrel with the New Divinity on God's sovereignty, he had no real argument with the idea of disinterested benevolence. The practical application of that concept had always been less Hopkins' idea of voluntary damnation than the idea that in loving God's creatures and creation, man loves and serves God. This latter idea rested on the importance of fruits in the establishment of God's Kingdom. It gave reality to the practice of mission and social reform. The Second Great Awakening is remembered less for its theology than its activity, because its theology required that activity.

Dwight was gratified by the fruits of this <u>Theology</u> at Yale and thence throughout New England. As students responded to his exhortations, Dwight tried to reduce the emotional aspect of the conversion process. He counseled young people under conviction to determine whether they were ready to enter God's service and abide by His will in all things. The path of piety was also the path of duty; religion was less an inward feeling of solitary devotion and mysticism than religious activity in daily life and a growing awareness of divine things.

Dwight and the majority of the New England clergy believed that the emotionalism of the First Great Awakening must not be repeated if the movement was to have credibility; and they were able to deflect that emotional energy into paths of social reform which would also hasten God's kingdom on earth.

The most prominent practitioner of Dwight's path of action was Lyman Beecher. Beecher arrived at Yale in 1793 presumably inclined toward religious matters despite the rationalist Yale atmosphere. During his first year the young man nearly died from scarlet fever. Dwight became president in Beecher's junior year; that same year, Beecher underwent conversion. Beecher noted that he had already chosen the ministry prior to conversion, a fact which probably bothered him. Conviction came from a chance remark of Beecher's stepmother that a passing drunk had once been under conviction. Beecher felt an impulse to pray, fell under conviction and proceeded to conversion in the classic Calvinist pattern.

> My convictions of sin were in accordance with my educational belief [strict Calvinism], and were deep and distressing, to the cutting off of all self-righteous hope from native excellence, or acceptable obedience in any action, social, civil, or religious, and laid me low in an agony of self despair, at the foot stool of mercy, as unholy, totally depraved, justly condemned, and hopeless of regeneration and pardon but through the infinite sovereign mercy of God, through the merits of Christ.[22]

While under conviction, Beecher read Edwards' Life of Brainerd as well as Edwards' theology and tracts, but later said he was converted in spite of them. Beecher's inspiration was Dwight.[23] Beecher graduated in 1797, but remained at Yale another year to study theology with Dwight, under whose tutelage Beecher read Hopkins, Bellamy and Andrew Fuller, an Englishman who taught that men were morally able to repent.

Beecher, as an old man, recalled his conversion and although he clearly favored Dwight over earlier Calvinists, it is unlikely that Beecher was as free from traditional Calvinism as he implied. Nevertheless, Dwight was a large figure in Beecher's life, perhaps because Dwight's theology diffused Beecher's inner confusion. This was a young man who had suffered continual rejection from his father seeking to grapple with an authoritarian religion.[24] If he were to accept the Edwardsean position on divine sovereignty, it would be difficult if not impossible to hope for acceptance and salvation. Dwight offered the choice of acceptance to Beecher. Given the choice, Beecher accepted God as he accepted his father. The difference was that God would accept Lyman Beecher as his father would not.

Beecher had received the glorious news of his salvation and accepted the duty of acting on it by spreading his experience to others. Beecher also accepted Dwight's position that religion must create virtuous and moral citizens, that the unsaved could still commit moral acts. The danger lay in becoming so concerned over one's individual salvation that the recipient failed to act upon it. "Do you not know, my friends, that you can not love, and be examining love at the same time? Some people, instead of getting evidence by <u>running</u> in the way of life, take a dark lantern and get down on their knees, and crowd on the boundary up and down, to make sure whether they have crossed it. If you want to make sure, run, and when you come in sight of the celestial city, and hear the songs of angels, then you'll know you're across."[25]

Beecher believed the problem of man's acceptance by God was at the center of religion. While he continued in the Calvinist tradition of man's accountability for his sins, and the inescapable fact that man could not choose to do good without the aid of the Spirit, Beecher also declared that despite man's accountability, God would only damn those who deliberately chose sin and rebellion. An Edwardsean would find little difference with this opinion, since without the Spirit man was incapable of choosing correctly, but Beecher found in favor of free will, and man's participation in his own salvation. Without this option revivals would be pointless, and Beecher, above all, was a revivalist. Theology was of little real use to him. Beecher strongly advocated the use of means, and to Beecher means were closely associated with, if not indistinguishable from, morality. The self could not become active without the moral character provided by religion. This same moral/religious education brought conversion. It was but a short step to public morality for its own sake. "I believe fully that we are no longer to trust Providence, and expect that God will indicate His cause while we neglect the use of appropriate means. God never has in this manner vindicated His cause; He never will."[26] Rather, Beecher asserted that conversion came from passively receiving religious education and acting upon it. Beecher advised those under conviction to get enough sleep, exercise and eat a balanced diet. They were not to fast or spend time in excessive prayer and introspection, because such activities led to depression and unwholesome mental excitement. They also led to the emotional release that Beecher rejected. Beecher defined a Christian as one with a wholesome, healthy outlook on life who demonstrated his love of Christ by imitation. The Christian obeyed God both externally and in his heart, and urged others to do likewise. He did not dwell on his state of salvation but turned to vigorous action in God's service.

In retrospect, one of the Beecher children stated that Lyman Beecher used his preaching to awaken men, answer their objections to the Gospel and show them a Gospel which was not at variance with common sense so that men could be led into an intelligent repentance.[27] What Beecher was doing differed little from Dwight's attack on the rationalists at Yale. Beecher took Dwight's concept of the use of means and developed it into the voluntary reform societies of the late eighteenth and early nineteenth centuries which would serve as the means. Reform and revival would inspire each other. By emphasizing man's free will to choose salvation, all men could and would be saved. Such a thought not only brought hope to those who felt incapable of achieving salvation under consistent Calvinism; it also fit the hope of the new republic and its cocky belief in itself.

Beecher arrived in Litchfield, Connecticut in 1810, shortly after the Reverend Dan Huntington led a revival that had converted three hundred. The call came from the influence of Judge Tapping Reeve, a founder of the Litchfield Law School. Reeve's first wife was a granddaughter of Jonathan Edwards, and Reeve was probably inclined toward a New Divinity outlook. Beecher came to the judge's attention through the efforts of two of Beecher's former tutors at Yale, Judge Gould of the law school and Sherman, who gave Judge Reeve a copy of Beecher's sermon on "The Government of God desirable" which had a definite Hopkinsian tone. After some investigation, Reeve influenced the selection of Beecher who was happy to accept.

When Beecher arrived, he found a rural town in a state of transition. There were numerous small businesses and many citizens participated in the textile industry by carding wool at home. The law school had a growing reputation as a improvement over reading law with an established attorney. Sarah Pierce had established her Female Academy, one of the earliest opportunities for female secondary education. In short, Litchfield was in a state of flux, and soon became a center for revival.

Beecher began preaching for a revival as soon as he arrived. He preached twice on Sundays, exhorted in the evenings and encouraged the deacons to pray for the revival. Within a year, Beecher wrote Asahel Hooker that after two or three excommunications to prove his intent of purifying the church, there were signs of an impending revival. When the revival came about in 1812, it lasted four years, not only in the town of Litchfield, but throughout that part of the state.

For Beecher, successful revivals were the first step on the road to voluntary associations and the millennium. Beecher originally conceived of voluntary associations as a weapon against disestablishment, though when he was unable to prevent that, Beecher declared that disestablishment had freed the voluntary associations from government influence.[28] For Beecher, the millennium would establish a society where both public opinion and law insured propriety, order and temperance, much like the early commonwealth of Massachusetts. Society could reach perfection, though human nature could not, hence the need for vigilance until the coming of the Kingdom. To this end more clergy were needed to spread the Gospel in a ratio of one clergyman per one thousand people. Hence, Beecher was active in the Charitable Society of Connecticut for the Education of Indigent, Pious Young Men for the Ministry of the Gospel, one of the earliest voluntary associations. It was but the beginning.

VI

Varying theological concepts of man's relationship to God and the assurance of salvation gave the missionaries a rather schizophrenic view of their respective individual states of grace. On one level they must surely be exemplifying an Edwardsian love of Being in general, a Hopkinsian practice of disinterested benevolence, a recognition of the importance of preaching to all as if all would be saved. Surely they had made the ultimate sacrifice as they followed God's call into the Hawaiian wilderness of unbelievers.

The presumption that those accepting the missionary call received the guarantee of salvation was bolstered by both theology and public opinion. Dwight and Beecher championed the cause of mission not only as a means of salvation, but also as the capstone of the voluntarysocieties, a focal point for the hopes of the public at large. Martha W. Bliss expressed this popular view in a letter to Elizabeth Edwards Bishop. "I feel," she wrote, "as though missionaries were those whom the Saviour delights to honor . . . . I know their station is enviable, even while I grieve for their sufferings. I trust," Martha Bliss continued, "that you live in the constant enjoyment of religion. I always feel as though the attainments of missionaries were vastly above those of common Christians. They appear much more dead to the world, & their affections more elevated."[29]

Unfortunately, doubts remained. The missionaries wondered if their choice was truly selfless. Unregenerate man would instinctively seek to avoid damnation by choosing salvation -- a choice which would have quite the opposite effect. Means alone were not enough; works not yielded by faith were insufficient. Doubt was rampant. After five years as a missionary in the Sandwich Islands, Levi Chamberlain lamented, "I do not read the Scripture with the Self-application that I once did. -- I have not a quick moral sense. I have hardened my heart to the fear of God. It is my belief that [I] have not yet surrendered my heart unto God. God is not in all my thoughts."[30]

If the missionaries who had the benefit of a strong theological and scriptural foundation suffered such doubts as to their own salvation, it is not to be wondered at that their requirements for an Hawaiian candidate's admission into the church were excessively strict. There was great concern that the efficacy of means not be confused with a true conversion, and that

the candidate be closely watched for the fruits of his
or her new regenerate state.

GOD'S SOVEREIGNTY: A THEOLOGICAL PROBLEM - ENDNOTES

1. The basic sources for this general discussion of
    Calvinism and the early development of the Puritan
    tradition are: Alan Simpson, Puritanism in Old and
    New England, (Chicago: University of Chicago Press,
    1955); William Warren Sweet, Religion in the
    Development of American Culture, 1765-1840, (New
    York: Charles Scribner's Sons, 1952); Perry Miller,
    "Preparation for Salvation in Seventeenth Century
    New England," in Nature's Nation, (Cambridge MA:
    The Belknap Press, 1967) 50-77; David D. Hall, The
    Faithful Shepherd: A History of the New England
    Ministry in the Seventeenth Century, (Chapel Hill:
    University of North Carolina Press, 1972). For
    information on the Calvinist concept of church and
    state, see: Michael Walzer, The Revolution of the
    Saints: A Study in the Origins of Radical Politics,
    (Cambridge MA: Harvard University Press, 1965).
    Source material pertaining to the theological
    response to the antinominian crisis may be found
    in: Sacvan Bercovitch, The American Jeremiad,
    (Madison: University of Wisconsin, 1978); James W.
    Jones, The Shattered Synthesis: New England
    Puritanism before the Great Awakening, (New Haven:
    Yale University Press, 1973).
        Arminianism was the doctrine of free will
    espoused by Jacobus Arminius in contrast to
    Calvinist predestination.

2. "And I will establish my covenant between me and
    thee and thy seed after thee in their generations
    for an everlasting covenant, to be a God unto thee,
    and to thy seed after thee."   (Genesis 17:7)

3. Source material for the Great Awakening was taken
    from Howard Frederick Vos, "The Great Awakening in
    Connecticut," (Ph.D. dissertation, Northwestern
    University, 1967); Edwin Scott Gaustad, The Great
    Awakening in New England, (New York: Harper &
    Brothers, 1957); Alan Heimert, Religion and the
    American Mind from the Great Awakening to the
    Revolution, (Cambridge MA: Harvard University
    Press, 1966).   For information referring
    specifically to Jonathan Edwards, see Clyde A.
    Holbrook, The Ethics of Jonathan Edwards: Morality
    and Aesthetics, (Ann Arbor: University of Michigan

50

Press, 1973); Perry Miller, <u>Jonathan Edwards</u>, (William Sloane Associates Inc., 1949).

4. Jonathan Edwards, "The Works of President Edwards," vol. 3, 9-23 in <u>The Great Awakening: The Beginnings of Evangelical Pietism in America</u>, ed. John M. Bumstead (Waltham MA: Blaisdell Publishing Company, 1970), p. 31.

5. George Whitefield quoted by Joseph Tracy, in <u>The Great Awakening</u> (1845; reprint, New York: Arno Press & New York Times, 1969), p. 105.

6. "Now unto the King eternal, immortal, invisible, the only wise God, be honour and glory for ever and ever. Amen. (I Timothy 1:17)

7. Jonathan Edwards quoted by Sydney E. Ahlstrom, in <u>A Religious History of the American People</u>, Vol. I (Garden City NY: Image Books, 1975), p. 368.

8. Edwards, "Justification by Faith Alone," in <u>The Great Awakening: Documents Illustrating the Crisis and Its Consequences</u>, ed. Alan Heimert and Perry Miller, (New York: Bobbs-Merril Company Inc., 1967), pp. 10-11, 13.

9. Ibid., p. 8.

10. Edwards, <u>Thoughts on the Revival of Religion in New England and the Way in which it Ought to be Acknowledged and Promoted</u>, (Northampton: Semeon Butler, 1819), p. 192.

11. Edwards, "A Treatise Concerning Religious Affections," in <u>The Great Awakening Documents</u>, pp. 518-520.

12. Ibid., pp. 254, 531-532, 535, 538.

13. Source material for the New Divinity was taken from: Frank Hugh Foster, <u>A Genetic History of the New England Theology</u>, (New York: Russell & Russell Inc., 1963); Heimert, <u>Religion and the American Mind</u>, op. cit. For information referring more specifically to Samuel Hopkins, see: Joseph A. Conforti, "Samuel Hopkins and the New Divinity: Theology, Ethics and Social Reform in Eighteenth Century New England," <u>William & Mary Quarterly</u>, 37

(1977): 572-589, and <u>Samuel Hopkins and the New Divinity Movement: Calvinism, the Congregational Ministry and Reform in New England Between the Great Awakenings</u>, (Grand Rapids: Christian University Press, 1981); Oliver Elsbree, "Samuel Hopkins and His Doctrine of Benevolence," <u>New England Quarterly</u>, VIII (December 1935): 534-550.

14. Quoted by Vos, pp. 112-113.

15. Quoted by Foster, p. 135.

16. Ibid., p. 155.

17. Ibid., pp. 110-111.

18. Kenneth Silverman, <u>Timothy Dwight</u>, (New York: Twayne Publishers Inc., 1969), pp. 95-96.

19. Timothy Dwight, <u>Theology; Explained and Defended</u>, (New Haven: T. Dwight & Sons, 1839), Vol. 3, p. 53.

20. Ibid., p. 68.

21. Ibid., p. 163.

22. Barbara Cross, ed., <u>The Autobiography of Lyman Beecher</u>, (Cambridge MA: The Belknap Press of Harvard University Press, 1961), Vol. 1, pp. 28-30; Lyman Beecher, <u>Views of Theology</u>, (Cincinnati: Truman and Smith, 1836), p. 154.

23. Cross, pp. 28-30.

24. Ibid., p. xii.

25. Ibid., p. 48.

26. Cross, p. 48.

27. Marie C. Caskey, "Faith and Theology in the Beecher Family," (Ph.D. dissertation, Yale University, 1974), p. 67.

28. In 1818 the Congregational church in Connecticut lost its favored position as the established, i.e., state supported, church of that state a position it had enjoyed since the founding of the colony. No longer could Congregational clergy from their

favored position collect monies or dictate social mores. Massachusetts and other New England states followed Connecticut's lead in disestablishing the Congregational church and voluntary associations became correspondingly more important.

29. Martha W. Bliss to Elizabeth Bishop, January 5, 1826, ML, HMCSL.

30. Levi Chamberlain, March 24, 1828, Journal, ML, HMCSL.

CHAPTER III

THE ROAD TO DAMASCUS

"And it came to pass, that, as I made my journey, and was come nigh unto Damascus about noon, suddenly there shone from heaven a great light round about me. And I fell unto the ground, and heard a voice saying unto me, Saul, Saul, why persecutest thou me? And I answered, Who art thou, Lord? And he said unto me, I am Jesus of Nazareth, whom thou persecutest. . . . And I said, what shall I do, Lord?" (The Acts of the Apostles 22:6-10)

Calvinist theology with its insistence that one must preach to all as if all would be saved inevitably brought up the issue of missionary work not only among the unregenerate of one's own culture, but also among those whose culture was an anathema to the average Calvinist. Seventeenth and eighteenth century missionary work among the American Indians established the model for nineteenth century missionary institutions. This preliminary work provided generic concepts of both "savage" unbelievers and heroic missionaries; it indicated what success might be expected and what obstacles needed to be overcome. The legacy of missionary journals and tracts also provided exciting but pious reading material for participants in the Second Great Awakening.

The problem of "otherness" preceded the work with the Indians and would remain as a hurdle no missionary ever fully overcame, regardless of his or her location. The "other," or "wild man" represented everything civilized culture did not, and the key to this "wildness" was the lack of anything resembling Judeo-Christian belief and culture. The "wild man" was pitied for his separateness and occasionally even admired for it as in the eighteenth century concept of the "noble savage." He could not distinguish from right and wrong, and so usually chose the wrong path, albeit innocently. Paradoxically, however, the "wild man" was also greatly feared. If the "wild man" was often depicted as one of nature's innocents, he was also an entity of physical and seductive power. Despite the "wild man's" alleged strength, however, he would suffer cultural struggle, some might say defeat, at the hands of "civilized" Europeans. The Calvinists subjected this "noble savage" to military, political and cultural dominance. Indeed, the Calvinists had no choice. If the "wild man" was truly human, truly innocent, then he was on a par with the Europeans. If the groups were equal, then the Europeans must recognize the "wildness" within themselves. Rather than encounter the "wild man" within, the Calvinists chose to project their own "wildness" onto the unbeliever, and then destroy those traits.[1]

From the seventeenth through the nineteenth centuries missionaries performed the bulk of this "rehabilitative" work. Those who became missionaries, whether or not they did so from evangelical commitment, were not typical of their culture. A missionary is an individual whose converting experience so solidifies the values of the subculture that his or her evangelical efforts not only serve the unbeliever but inspire the general culture. This phenomenon was very evident in the experience of the voluntary societies of the early nineteenth century as the general believing public placed missionary activity at the pinnacle of religious commitment.[2]

The example of the early missionaries to Hawai'i continued as an inspiration throughout the nineteenth century. Writing for a Honolulu audience in 1866, William Ellis reminded his readers of the exemplary traits of the pioneers with whom he had served, "I often marked and admired their unobtrusive piety, and their persevering conscientious attention to all the great objects of their Mission, their simple style of living, the absence among them of self-seeking and self-indulgence, and their self-consecration to their sacred work."[3]

Puritan ideas about the need for missionary activity were both a natural outgrowth and a key element of their religious experience. As early as the sixteenth century, Puritan concepts of the millennium stressed that both Jews and Gentiles would be converted in the latter days and indicated that until these conversions occurred, the millennium would not take place. Christ would not come until three requirements had been met: first, the conversion of unbelievers; second, the gathering of the believers within the church, and third, the political rule of Christ occurring as Christian men gained office. It was with such criteria in mind that the Puritans built the city on the hill in Boston.

On a more personal, individual level, Puritan theology also recognized man's utter loss without God's grace and the impossibility of salvation without Him as problems needing resolution. All people were the same in their need for grace, and love for the sinners dictated that efforts be made to convert them. Those who were not told of the Gospel would surely perish, and just as surely come back in the day of judgement to accuse the lukewarm Christian who would not exert himself or herself on their behalf.

Calvinists could not avoid the injunction that they must evangelize unbelievers whoever and wherever they were. For the seventeenth century Puritans, the primary missionary field was among the American Indians. In the early nineteenth century the American Board would work with unbelievers in Asia and the Middle East as well as the Hawaiians. The Calvinists would have their greatest impact among the Indians and the Hawaiians, the two peoples whose "wildness" was most feared. Among both nations the Calvinists missionaries would use the means of education to spread the values of a literate culture thereby irrevocably separating these two indigenous peoples from the richness of their respective oral traditions. Those accepting literacy would be separated from traditional society and inducted into a new culture. Efforts among the Indians created separately designated communities of "praying Indians" ravaged by both sides during King Philip's War (1675). In Hawai'i, however, the entire nation became part of the new society proffered by the missionaries.[4]

II

The first challenge the English colonists had to face in connection with the Indians was to define who or what the these people were and what their relationship to the colonists was. Before leaving England, the future settlers determined that the defeat of the

Spanish armada in 1588 gave the English the obligation to proselytize unbelievers to the Protestant faith. The colonial charters of Virginia, Plymouth, Massachusetts Bay and Connecticut all established missionary work among non-Christians as a primary objective of the respective colonies.[5]

Upon arrival in 1630 the Puritans soon concluded that God had reduced the indigenous Indian population in order to clear a place for his Elect. Between 1616 and 1617 a plague of unknown origin had removed about one-third of the Indian population between Narragansett Bay and the Penobscot River. Such losses altered the balance of power and a series of Indian wars ensued, further thinning out the Indian population. Later, a smallpox outbreak affected the Indians near Massachusetts Bay (1633-1634). It was clear to the Puritans that the Indians did not enjoy God's favor.

The Pilgrims who had preceded their Calvinist brethren at Massachusetts Bay by ten years had definite ideas of whose favor the Indians did enjoy. Though aware of their obligation to bring Christianity to the heathen, the Pilgrims believed that a failure of the Indians to respond to such overtures clearly placed the natives in the enemy camp where they could be despised every bit as much as the Israelites had despised the Philistines. The Pilgrims would be fair with the Indians, but would not trust them.

The Puritans took the idea of their commitment to evangelize the Indians more seriously, and, consequently, had to reach some sort of <u>modus operandi</u>. Though the colony's leadership lacked any sort of plan, and had presented the idea of missionary activity more

as a means of gaining their colonial charter than
anything else, the problem of Indian unbelief remained,
both as a religious and a legal issue. The legal
question was easier to solve. The courts gave the
Indians protection from exploitation and forbade the
purchase of Indian land without permission. The
government licensed all trade with the Indians to
protect them from the evils of liquor and guns. Aware
of the colony's failure to embark on extensive
missionary efforts, the Massachusetts Bay General Court
required all Indians under its jurisdiction to attend
Sunday religious instruction (1644) and set aside lands
for "praying Indian" communities (1646).

The problem with this public commitment to convert
the Indians was that the Puritans would have to concede
that Indians were fully human, i.e., capable of becoming
regenerate. In so doing, the Puritans had to admit that
they, themselves, were subject to the same
uncontrollable impulses the Indians gave way to so
freely. Convinced that left to their own devices the
Indians would worship the devil, the Puritans found
three plausible explanations for the apparent inferior
status of the Indians, in order to free themselves from
the spectre of possible spiritual equality. The Indians
might be seen as children of the human race whose
passions were, as yet, unrestrained by reason; as beings
whose enslavement to their passions made them little
better than animals, or, the more promising idea that
the Indians might merely be lacking the arts of western
civilization.

The question of whether the Indians were educable
was of key importance for a group whose culture was

synonymous with literacy. The Puritans hoped it was lack of education that made the Indians so different. In order for the gospel to flourish among the Indians, they must be taught the social, cultural, moral, intellectual and religious values of Puritan society. This would be difficult to do unless the prospective converts could be isolated from the influences of their natural environment. After the Pequots and the Narragansetts were subdued (1637 and 1643, respectively), the circumstances for such an environmental experiment were auspicious.

The problems of differentness and unbelief could both be solved by isolating potential converts in separate communities. In these "praying towns" the Indians could be educated in the arts of western civilization. As they learned to live like Europeans, the Indians would be better able
to comprehend the precepts of the Christian religion. Conversion would be the final touch, assimilating the Indians into European culture and removing their more threatening aspects.

According to John Eliot, the most well-known missionary of his time, the first task of the Puritan missionary was to gather the Indians together into "civilized" life in order to provide the necessary external preparation for conversion. The Indians would learn the rudiments of western civilization through disciplined, rigorous training. The men would learn to farm, and women would learn the domestic arts. Both sexes would become literate and so broaden the gap between the praying Indians and their traditional culture. At Natick the Indians learned to build English houses, follow English law, wear English clothing and reject Indian culture.

Indian children attended school, and received a more complete education in European ways by serving in the colonists' homes. In the late 1630s several Indian children lived in Massachusetts Bay as apprentices and servants, but, on the whole, the program was not successful. Colonists were often hesitant about taking Indians into their homes, and Indian parents were loath to part from their children. The idea of bringing indigenous children into American homes was revived in the nineteenth century by the American Board in the mission fields of India and Hawai'i with similar, unfavorable results.[6]

The Puritans might have had greater success if they had not demanded such a change in Indian lifestyle, but the colonists believed the Indian must undergo the same process of conversion as any Puritan, and, therefore, must understand the Bible and creed in an English context. The Indians were taught the virtues of submission and dependence, to shun evil and feel guilt for any association with it. Indians were taught to be passive and to follow the rules of church and society. In the "Conclusion and Orders" drawn up at Concord in 1647 several sachems condemned drunkenness, powwowing (i.e., the practice of traditional religion), lying, stealing, polygamy, enmity, the picking and eating of lice, body grease, fornication, adultery, murder, howling at funerals and wifebeating. The sachems enjoined their people to seek God, use their time well, be humble, pay their debts to the English, keep the Sabbath, wear their hair in the English fashion and pray. The Hawaiians would draw similar conclusions from their missionary contact.[7]

The methods and rationale of the Puritan missionaries would be widely imitated by their nineteenth century counterparts. The best known of the seventeenth century missionaries were the Mayhews and John Eliot. The Reverend Thomas Mayhew, Jr. began working with the Indians at Martha's Vineyard in 1642, winning his first convert the following year. Mayhew had one hundred ninety-nine converts by 1651.[8] After his son died in 1657, Thomas Mayhew, Sr. continued the work. The Mayhews worked at Martha's Vineyard for five generations until 1803. They stressed conversion before civilization and did not separate believing Indians from the unbelieving. But Martha's Vineyard was isolated, and the Indians did not resist the Mayhews' efforts.

The Mayhews were more successful in maintaining their converts, but John Eliot was the better known missionary. Between 1643 and 1671 Eliot published eleven pamphlets to gain the interest and support of the English public for his evangelism efforts. In 1646 the Massachusetts legislature passed an act for the propagation of the gospel among the Indians. That October Eliot and three companions went to Nonantum at the invitation of one Waaubon. Eliot preached a one and one-half hour sermon and was invited to return.

Eliot established several missionary themes which would be replayed in the Hawaiian field. Eliot perceived that although the Indians were on the lowest rung of the ladder of civilization, they were also both educable and redeemable by the grace of God. Eliot told the Indians that there were only two basic differences between themselves and the English: "First, we know, serve, and pray unto God, and they doe not; Secondly, we labour and work in building, planting, clothing ourselves . . . and they doe not."[9]

Eliot worked on the basis of three Calvinist principles. The first was God's sovereignty by which He drew those who had lost true knowledge into the Elect; second, preaching was the means of redemption, and third, everyone, could respond to preaching. Eliot believed that once the Indian candidates had been organized into satisfactory political units, they should be joined into a church. In this he was frustrated by the Roxbury elders, and the church at Natick was not established until 1660.

Eliot also strove to preach to the Indians in their own language which was difficult, given the many dialects of Algonquian, but as he translated the Bible and wrote pamphlets, the language became more standardized. Eliot did more translation work than any American missionary before the nineteenth century.

There were fourteen settlements of "praying Indians" in 1675 with a total population of three thousand six hundred (about twenty percent of the total Indian population) organized into twenty-four Indian churches.[10] These same Indians would be decimated by both sides during King Philip's War (1675), a particularly grisly event noted for its atrocities. During and after the war the majority of colonists subscribed to the view that all Indians should be held under the utmost suspicion, thus diminishing the appeal of missionary work among the Indians.

After the war, Cotton Mather, a commissioner of the New England Company, tried to keep the missionary spirit alive by pointing out that until God's kingdom arrived, people should strive to create as much of it as they could under their existing circumstances. Converting Indians was a part of this effort. Samuel Sewall agreed, asserting that there would be no kingdom without the conversion of the Indians. Most Puritans, however, took little interest in missionary efforts. No new impetus to mission would be felt until the First Great Awakening.

The First Great Awakening produced perhaps the best known of the American missionaries who also served as a role model for later missionaries. Heavily influenced by Jonathan Edwards, and immortalized by him, David Brainerd was a living example of the Edwardsean love of Being in general. Brainerd was the missionary prototype. David Brainerd came from a pious family; two of his brothers also joining the ministry. As a youth Brainerd underwent a protracted conviction/conversion experience while studying for the ministry under his brother, Nehemiah. It began in 1738 and did not conclude until 1739 when Brainerd was twenty-one. The description of the event became a model for those under conviction during the Second Great Awakening.

Brainerd's conviction began on a "Sabbath-day Morning" as he "was walking out in some secret Duties" when it pleased God "to give me on a Sudden such a Sense of my Danger and the Wrath of God, that I stood amazed, and my former good Frames . . . all presently vanished; and from the View, that I had of my Sin and Vileness, I was much distressed all that Day, fearing the Vengeance of God would soon overtake me; I was much dejected, and kept much alone, and sometimes begrutched [sic] the Birds and Beasts their Happiness, because they were not exposed to eternal Misery, as I evidently saw I was." Finally, on July 12, 1739, after much distress, as Brainerd was walking in a grove "unspeakable Glory seemed to open to the View and Apprehension of my Soul: I don't mean any external Brightness . . . nor do I intend any Imagination of a Body of Light . . . or any Thing of that Nature; but it was a new inward Apprehension . . . that I had of God, such as I never had before . . . . And my Soul rejoyced with Joy unspeakable, to see such a God."[11]

Three years later Brainerd "began to find it sweet to pray; and could think of undergoing the greatest sufferings in the cause of Christ, with pleasure; and found myself willing . . . to suffer banishment from my native land, among the heathen, that I might do something for their salvation."[12] In November 1742 the Society in Scotland for Propagation of Christian Knowledge accepted Brainerd as a missionary to the Indians.

It was not an easy life. In 1743 Brainerd confided to his journal, "My circumstances are such that I have no comfort of any kind, but what I have in God. I live in the most lonesome wilderness." Two years later Brainerd confessed that after an attack of depression, he returned to his missionary labors at "peace in my own soul; and was satisfied, that if not one of the Indians should be profited by my preaching, but they should all be damned, yet I should be accepted and rewarded as faithful."[13] Four months later (from June 1745 to July

1747) Brainerd was gratified to lead his Indians in a revival, baptizing seventy-seven the first eleven months.

Brainerd left the mission field only as a result of disease. The evangelist had suffered from tuberculosis since his college days at Yale, and his life of deprivation and hardship further weakened his health. Brainerd spent the remaining year of his life in the Jonathan Edwards household, nursed by Edwards' daughter, Jerusha, until his death in 1747 at the age of thirty. The couple were engaged and exposure to Brainerd's illness made Jerusha Edwards her fiancee's partner in death, if not in life.

Jonathan Edwards was deeply moved by his guest's piety and dedication to God. At Edwards' urging, Brainerd consented to the publication of his journal. The Life and Diary of David Brainerd edited by Jonathan Edwards enjoyed immediate popularity until well into the nineteenth century. In an age and region bereft of light reading, Brainerd's story offered the chaste romance of David Brainerd and Jerusha Edwards. For those of a more theological bent, the publication clearly marked Brainerd as one fulfilling the Edwardsean ideal. Edwards commended Brainerd's life to all who would claim a relationship to God as an exemplary model of the true Christian lifestyle. "To Missionaries in particular," Edwards wrote of Brainerd, "may his example of labouring, praying, denying himself, and enduring hardness with unfainting resolution and patience, and his faithful, vigilant, and prudent conduct in many other aspects, offered instruction." Indeed, Dr. Leonard Woods, the Abbot Professor at Andover

Theological Seminary, later wrote that to neglect to read Brainerd's life was to experience a loss in the permanent advancement of the potential reader's holiness and future usefulness in the ministry. Joseph Tracy noted that Brainerd's journal and biography were extensively read, producing a deep and permanent impression on the Christian world.[14]

The Life and Diary of David Brainerd fulfilled these roles, because it provided a flesh and blood model of Edwardsean theology and missionary success; albeit a success overshadowed by incredible hardship. But to the readers, especially youthful ones, it proved that good could overcome evil, that the pious youth could gain the love of a desirable, young woman, and, of course, that the good die young. Here was no nuts and bolts descriptions of missionary pragmatism, but a glimpse into the soul of one of God's chosen. It was the epitome of Edwardsean sensationalism.

Brainerd was not the only missionary to the Indians during the First Great Awakening. Work among the Indians offered the converted another option for the expression of their love of God. John Sargeant labored in Stockbridge, Eleazer Wheelock at the Moor's Indian Charity School (later, Dartmouth) and two of Brainerd's brothers, David and John, on the Pennsylvania frontier. But these were less introspective men, or at least less given to confiding their thoughts to published journals, and so evoked little public acclaim. Jonathan Edwards, himself, after his dismissal from Northampton, turned down the invitation of Scottish clerics to join them, choosing instead to serve the Indians at Stockbridge. Here Edwards produced his best systematic theology, though less for the Indians' edification than for that of the New Divinity men. Yet, Edwards' presence at Stockbridge clearly demonstrated his commitment to the missionary cause and provided the New Divinity men with an example of a calling where one could remain ascetic, altruistic and piously pure.

The basic theological, practical, romantic and altruistic impetus for missionary work was now in place. Eliot and Mayhew had proven that it could be done. The theology of the millennium, Edwardsean love of Being in general and Hopkinsian disinterested benevolence proved that it must be done. Brainerd had demonstrated who must do it. The missionary cause was a Christian duty in which all Christians had a part. However, the missionary calling was for special people whose faith and commitment set them apart as people chosen by God to serve as an example for both the unbelievers and their Christian brethren.

III

Missionary work whether among the Indians or anyone else could only occur as a fruit of the conversion experience. This mysterious process was the key indicator of salvation in the Reformed tradition regardless of one's original cultural affiliation. Among the Puritans, the candidate received grace passively with no true injunction to act upon it. Edwardsean theology made an active response more than a little desirable. The Hopkinsian and New Divinity approach as interpreted by Dwight and Beecher made action an imperative response verifying the candidate's new state of grace.

The testimony of Edwards, Brainerd, Beecher and other sources provided individuals caught in the Second Great Awakening with a clear indication of what a conversion experience was and what it required. The ambiguity of disinterested benevolence, however, precluded the relief of certainty. As Clarissa Lyman wrote her parents:

> The most important yet the most difficult duty we are called to perform is the duty of self-denial. It is easy to profess an attachment to the Redeemer's cause. It is easy to do many things which he commands; - but to sanctify the corrupt passions of the heart, and cheerfully and unreservedly to surrender all we have to the service of Christ is a task so difficult that the grace of God alone can enable a sinner to perform it. . . . I do not consider the mere act of giving up the world as evidence of piety. It is much easier to give up the world than to give up the heart to God.[15]

Several of the men and women who volunteered for the mission field recorded their conversion experience and its immediate affect on respective lives. Hiram Bingham made a public profession of faith at the Congregational Church of Christ at Bennington, Vermont in 1811 at the age of twenty-two. That "spiritual season of divine searching" changed the direction of Hiram's life from farming to God's service. "God had crowned my life with undeserved mercies, he then blest me with a good constitution and good health, & with mediocrity of talents, & as I was led to believe, had given me a desire to serve him in the gospel of his Son"[16] Apparently, the Bingham family was accustomed to the effect of spiritual seasons; among Hiram's five brothers, two became ministers, and two, doctors.

Samuel Ruggles at about the age of thirteen "began to feel that I was a dependent creature, and to reflect on the goodness of God towards me, since I was bereft of earthly parents. This led me to think upon myself and to consider my heart, which I found full of iniquity, ingratitude and guilt. About this time it pleased God in his infinite mercy and rich grace . . . to bare my will and make me choose Christ.[17] The experience inspired Ruggles to seek an education, and by 1817 he had determined on a missionary career, concerned that if he was not chosen soon, he would have to go into business to alleviate his poor financial condition.

Levi Chamberlain made perhaps the greatest change in lifestyle when he met Christ, for he had been a successful businessman. Levi began to think seriously about religion at age seventeen, when he was afflicted with the health problem of "raising blood." The young man concluded that "God has arrested me in the progress of evil by depriving me of health" thus demonstrating the fleeting quality of life. "God grant that I may profit by his wise dispensations."[18]

Meanwhile, Chamberlain received secular profits in partnership with Jesse Holbrook. In 1817 the two opened a Boston mercantile devoted to the buying and selling of European, Indian and American products. Levi became a heavy donor to missions and other philanthropic causes. Then in September 1818, Levi Chamberlain's life changed.

One morning Christ "appeared to be the centre point the grand focus where the Spirit concentrates the only visible amidst invisible," Chamberlain wrote, "I could conceive of him as standing between heaven and earth."

In response to this vision, Chamberlain desired "to give up myself soul and body to [Christ] . . . to renounce all other lords, all other masters . . . . I do desire to give him my whole heart & to keep nothing. back, my temporal substance is his to be used in his service." Two days later Levi Chamberlain joined the church and recorded,

> This is a day which will be eternally remembered, for on this day in the presence of God, angels and men I came forward and solemnly took upon me the vows of God & gave myself up in a public manner & had the ordinance of baptism administered & partook of the sacrament. By these solemn ordinances I have professedly become the Servant of Christ. I have pledged myself to be faithful to his course and promised never to dishonor it. I profess to have experienced a change of ieart, to depend on the agency of the Spirit to carry on the work untill my sanctification be complete & untill I shall arrive to the fulness of the stature of a perfect man in Christ. And now I have put my hand to the plow & I cannot go back, henceforth the eye of the world is upon me.[19]

William Chamberlain commented to his young relative "You observed to me in a letter sometime since that your views respecting religion were altered - you was never an infidel, but no doubt thought it of far less importance then it really is, or as you may now deem it to be, even the first concern."[20] Levi Chamberlain embarked on a year of serious prayer and soul searching with the assistance of Christian friends, confiding, "It has pleased that infinite God . . . greatly to exercise my mind about the concerns of my soul. I hope I have been enabled to see something of the evils of sin & of the desperate wickedness of my heart; to believe that the heart must be renewed by divine grace . . . . And it has pleased this same Almighty Being, at length to enable me to hope in his mercy." Chamberlain began to wonder "what will be the natural result of [his] attachment" to Jesus, and about his lack of spirituality and faith. At length Levi decided to give up his mercantile business to seek an education, and began a course at Andover Theological Seminary, but was, at twenty-nine, too old to complete the full course. Chamberlain reflected that although "I once thought that I was bound by no tie to my fellow creatures stronger [than] that which obliged me to pay my just debts, and to conform to the rules of moral honesty . . . . I was brought to see . . . that I was a lost sinner . . . and was involved in the condemnation of a violated holy law . . . and finally that if I was ever saved it must be through faith in the merits & atonement of Christ, then I felt that God had a right to my services, that my fellow creatures had claims upon me."[21]

Levi Chamberlain applied to the American Board of Commissioners for Foreign Missions to serve the Indians. Instead he became the assistant to Samuel Worcester, and later joined the Second Company to the Sandwich Islands. Chamberlain did not seek his "own good or glory; but the advancement of the Redeemer's kingdom, I ask not for ease or long life . . . . Let me spend my strength in disinterested efforts to do good."[22]

William Richards took a more direct path to Christian commitment. He felt his first inkling of "Christian hope" in 1808 at the age of fifteen and made public profession three years later. Richard's oldest brother, James, a graduate of Williams College (1809) and Andover Theological Seminary (1812); a founder of the American Board, and missionary to Ceylon (Sri Lanka) until his death in 1822 had a strong influence on the young man's life and career choice. William followed in his brother's footsteps in both education and vocation. Shortly after his arrival at Williams College, William wrote his father, "I have never since I commenced studying with a view to preparations for the ministry wished . . . to relinquish it. . . . It seems to me that in a stronger manner than ever I wish to devote myself to the cause of Christ."[23]

Female missionaries generally expressed far more emotion and even desperation in their conversion experiences. Sybil Moseley falling under conviction at the age of nineteen, did not believe in the efficacy of means. "Not everyone that talks of Religion - not everyone that is less attached to the world on account of afflictions - not everyone that exhorts others to seek the salvation of their Souls - not everyone that prays has had their Sins forgiven . . . but will be cast into outer darkness. Will not that be my doom? Am I not vainly imagining I love religion? Can the Saviour love the holy government of God, when in reality I do not?" Sybil received a converting experience, but did not fully trust her ability to repent. On January 15, 1812 she recorded "I have, in the presence of Men, of Angels, and of my Maker, entered into a most solemn and everlasting covenant to be the Lords [sic] . . . . I was enabled in some means to feel my unworthiness, and through divine grace, in some degree to rejoice in the Lord." But despite this assurance, "I wander, will ever love to wander" from God's blessings. Three years later, Sybil reflected on her service to God. "Oh! how little have I brought forth." To rectify this situation, Sybil expended much energy and prayer to encourage a revival at her school in western New York, but to no avail, "I leave my school without witnessing what I had anticipated."[24]

Clarissa Lyman began to meditate on her sinful condition at the age of twelve, but for ten years was unable to renounce the world. "The possibility that the Bible might prove true often disturbed my carnal security and caused me to tremble." At sixteen, she determined "to make a more vigorous effort and if unsuccessful never to disturb myself with regard to the future." After much study and prayer, Clarissa's "understanding" was convinced and she accepted Christ as fulfilling God's Law.[25]

Conversion changed Clarissa Lyman's life. "When I professed my faith in Christ - and my allegiance to him, I felt that I was no longer my own." After reflecting on God's grace, "I felt that no sacrifice would be considered too great to make for the promotion of his word." She was sure that if her sacrifice was to be in the missionary field, all obstacles would disappear.[26]

The converting experience with its call to action did not require its participants to embark on a foreign mission. Indeed, the ministerial leadership of the Second Great Awakening in New England was more concerned with building the citizenship virtues of a new republic and reaching the unchurched on the frontier that with the fate of unbelievers in foreign climes. For those individuals who wanted to work with another culture, there remained work among the Indians.

Foreign missionary activity, like the phenomena of the revivals themselves, was a grassroots movement. In the face of public enthusiasm the ministerial leadership quickly saw the potential of such interest as an ideal conversion fruit. The foreign missionary enterprise served to unify the conglomerate of emerging voluntary societies, bringing them all under its romantic glow.

THE ROAD TO DAMASCUS - ENDNOTES

1. See Hayden White, "The Forms of Wildness: Archaeology of an Idea," in The Wild Man Within: An Image of Western Thought from the Renaissance to Romanticism, ed. Edward Dudley & Maximillian E. Novak (Pittsburgh: University of Pittsburgh Press, 1972). Henri Baudet, Paradise on Earth: Some Thoughts on European Images of Non-European Man (New Haven: Yale University Press, 1965).

2. G. Gordon Brown, "Missionaries and Cultural Diffusion," American Journal of Sociology 50 (November 1944), 214-219.

3. William Ellis, The American Mission in the Sandwich Islands, a Vindication and an Appeal to the Proceedings of the Reformed Catholic Mission at Honolulu (Honolulu HI: H.M. Whitney, 1866), p. 17.

4. For a discussion of the effect literacy can have on a society, see, J. C. Carothers, "Culture, Psychiatry and the Written Word," Psychiatry 22 (November 1959), 307-320.

5. Alden T. Vaughan, New England Frontier: Puritans and Indians 1620-1675 (Boston: Little, Brown and Company, 1965), pp. 21-22.

6. Maria Loomis expressed the disillusionment of the mission family in Hawai'i when she commented that "living so near the village as we do, it is impossible to keep those [native children] in our family from their former associates. I regret very much that our situation nor the genius of the people among [whom] we dwell will not admit to taking children . . . with any hopes of success at present."
September 1, 1822, Journal, JC, HMCSL.

7. The earliest official code of laws in Hawai'i was proclaimed on December 8, 1827. There were three laws prohibiting murder, theft and adultery. Three other proposed laws prohibited rum selling, prostitution and gambling; their proclamation was postponed so that people would have time to understand them. Ralph Kuykendall, The Hawaiian Kingdom, op. cit., pp. 117-132.

8. Williston Walker, <u>Ten New England Leaders</u> (1901; reprint, New York: Arno Press, 1969), pp. 164-165.

9. Sidney H. Rooy, <u>The Theology of Missions in the Puritan Tradition</u> (Grand Rapids: William B. Eerdmans Publishing Co., 1965), p. 191.

10. Joseph Tracy, "History of the American Board of Commissioners for Foreign Missions" <u>History of the American Missions to the Heathen from their Commencement to the Present Time</u> (Worcester: Spooner & Howland, 1840), p. 14. James A. DeJong, <u>As the Waters Cover the Sea: Millennial Expectations in the Rise of Anglo-American Missions 1640-1810</u> (J.H. Kok N.V. Kampen, 1970), p. 46.

11. Jonathan Edwards, <u>The Life of David Brainerd</u> (New York: American Tract Society, n.d.), pp. 12, 24-25.

12. Ibid., p. 34.

13. Ibid., pp. 64-65, 121.

14. Ibid., pp. 356-357.

15. Clarissa Lyman, letter to her parents, Sept. 20, 1822, ML, HMCSL.

16. Hiram Bingham to Samuel Worcester, July 18, 1819, ML, HMCSL.

17. Samuel Ruggles to Rev. Samuel Wooster, Jan. 7, 1817, and to Jeremiah Evarts, Sept. 26, 1821, ML, HMCSL.

18. Levi Chamberlain, Oct. 19, 1815, Journal, JC, HMCSL.

19. Ibid., Sept. 3, 5, 1818.

20. Ibid.; Levi Chamberlain had both a father and a brother named William. William Chamberlain to Levi Chamberlain, Oct. 20, 1818, ML, HMCSL.

21. L. Chamberlain to Jeremiah Evarts, Sept. 26, 1821; to brother, George Chamberlain, Jan. 19, 1819, ML, HMCSL. Nov. 13, 1819, Journal, JC, HMCSL.

22. Ibid, Sept. 18, 1822.

23. Quoted by Samuel Williston, <u>William Richards</u> (Cambridge MA: Privately Printed, 1938) p. 8.

24. Sybil Moseley Bingham, Nov. 1, 1811; Jan. 15, 1812, Jan. 1, 1815 and Sept. 5, 1815, Journal, JC, HMCSL.

25. Clarissa Richards to parents, Sept. 20, 1822, ML, HMCSL.

26. Ibid.

CHAPTER IV

THE MACEDONIAN CALL

"And a vision appeared to Paul in the night;
There stood a man of Macedonia, and prayed
him, saying, Come over into Macedonia, and
help us. And after he had seen the vision,
immediately we endeavoured to go into
Macedonia, assuredly gathering that the Lord
had called us for to preach the gospel unto
them." (The Acts of the Apostles 16:9-10)

Americans, caught up in the excitement of founding
a new nation, were not the first to discover foreign
mission. That distinction belonged to the British who
launched the movement with the founding of the London
Missionary Society in 1795. It was not surprising that
the British developed a parallel interest in evangelism.
They, too, suffered from the effects of revolution,
though of a more technological nature. British clerics
were aware of the need to assert Christian values in an
increasingly secular society, and came to the conclusion
that to preserve the social order they must save
Christianity as the basis of society. British religious
leaders turned to foreign mission with much the same
needs and effect as their American cousins. In fact,
the British movement for evangelism and foreign mission
was a direct outgrowth of Edwardsean theology as it had
filtered through the Scottish church.

The rhetoric of English missions and the news of
actual British missionary activities greatly influenced
the American commitment to such a large project. London
Missionary Society sermons began appearing in the United

States in 1797. Copies had been sent to the Reverend Alexander McLean in Maine and were reprinted for an enthusiastic reception, especially among divinity students. Melville Horne's Letters on Mission appealed to a broader audience including Harriet Tiffany Stewart. Horne was a British chaplain at Sierra Leone, and the book consists of letters he wrote British clergymen arguing for the need of mission work at home and abroad. The Christian Researcher in Asia by the Reverend Claudius Buchanan, a Scottish Episcopalian who worked in India for twelve years, was an American bestseller during the War of 1812, and not only awakened further American interest in missionary work, but also added to the controversy over the war.

The news of actual mission fields was also widely read by the American public. The first issue of the Panoplist which began publication in 1805 carried stories about the London Missionary Society's work in South Africa among the Hottentots, in Ceylon (Sri Lanka), in Surat (in western India) and in Tahiti as well as news of a British Baptist mission in Bengal. The first mention made of the Sandwich Islands in the Panoplist occurred in 1808. In an article reprinted from the Evangelical Magazine, the newspaper reported that in 1806 a ship's captain had informed two missionaries in Tahiti of the presence of Isaac Davis and John Young in the Sandwich Islands and the advances these men had made in civilizing the islands over the past fifteen years. "How happy should we be to add, they have also the privilege of hearing and knowing the joyful sound of the gospel!" the editors exclaimed.[1]

The New Divinity men recognized missionary work as both the natural outgrowth of the revival and as a sign of the latter days, since God's kingdom could not arrive until all peoples had heard the gospel, repented, converted and lived lives of disinterested benevolence. As early as 1799, Hopkins was able to note five missionary societies, four of these Edwardsean in outlook. Jonathan Edwards, the Younger, Benjamin Trumbull, Samuel Hopkins, Timothy Dwight and Lyman Beecher all took an active interest in the establishment and work of missionary societies.

Timothy Dwight was a founding member of the Connecticut Missionary Society in 1798, donating $1000 to the cause. Using the London Missionary Society as a model and aware of their proximity to the American frontier, the membership of the Connecticut Missionary Society pledged themselves to Christianize the Indians and to promote Christian knowledge among the new settlements of the frontier. Efforts to work with the Indians proved too costly, however, and were set aside in 1803 until the American Board pledged itself to the Indian field.

The Massachusetts Missionary Society began the following year with Samuel Hopkins serving as vice-president. The society was primarily concerned with reaching settlers on the frontier and sent missionaries to Maine, New Hampshire, Vermont, Rhode Island, Ohio and Illinois armed with Bibles and religious tracts. By 1824 the society would sponsor two hundred twenty-four full time missionaries. Such a large enterprise required funds, and the Massachusetts Missionary Society provided a model for the umbrella organization the American Board became. To publicize their work the society founded the <u>Massachusetts Missionary Magazine</u> in 1803 which later merged with the <u>Panoplist</u>. In 1802 the first Cent Society began at Boston, collecting one cent each week from its members for the missionary cause. The ladies were also enlisted into an auxiliary, the Boston Female Society for Promoting the Diffusion of Christian Knowledge.

To provide spiritual nourishment the monthly Concert of Prayer was revitalized. The concert had begun in Scotland in 1744 and had been adopted by Jonathan Edwards with the idea that on a given day all good Christians would unite in their prayers for the revival. The concert was revived by the English Baptists in 1784, then by the London Missionary Society in 1795, and finally by the missionary societies of the United States as a day when Christians would unite their concerns for the success of the missionary cause. The Concert of Prayer would have a special significance for missionaries in the field, alleviating their sense of isolation and frustration.

On February 3, 1823 Clarissa Richards knew that on that particular day "the Christian world are praying for us, & for that cause which we profess to have near our hearts . . . . Could they be made sensible how liable we are to sink into a state of apathy without this intelligence to invigorate our dying faith . . . . Surely they would not be cold and heartless in these petitions this evening. But . . . they would use importunity in pleading for blessings, not only on those who have devoted themselves to the work of evangelizing the heathen, but, that happy day may be hastened when the kingdom of this world shall become the peaceable kingdom of our Lord."[2] Charles Stewart reflected that April 7, 1823 had also been the day of the Concert of Prayer. "While the burden of our petitions, . . . was 'Thy kingdom come!' the objects, and the end, of the Missionary cause rose with all their moral sublimity on our view." Stewart believed that every such service must effect the heart believing in prayer, "especially on that of the Missionary, who, however unknown, however solitary and destitute, still feels that he is included among the scattered bands for whose special blessing the followers of Christ unitedly bend their knees and lift their hands in prayer."[3]

The training of ministers was of great concern to the New Divinity men and the problem was especially acute in Massachusetts. In 1805 the Hollis Professorship of Divinity at Harvard College had gone to the Liberal, Henry Ware; Liberals were also appointed to four other chairs. In response, Jedidiah Morse, an Old Calvinist, facilitated the establishment of a seminary focusing on consistent Calvinism at Andover. Morse had long been active in the cause of missions among the Indians, serving in both the Massachusetts Missionary Society and the Society for the Propagation of the Gospel among the Indians and Others of North America. Morse had also begun the Panoplist as a newspaper promoting Christian orthodoxy.

Prior to the loss of Harvard to the Liberals, other consistent Calvinists had made plans for a seminary and lined up three wealthy backers; William Bartlett, giving $30,000; Moses Brown, giving $10,000; and John Norris, giving $10,000. Samuel Abbott gave $20,000 to endow a professor of theology and left a legacy of $100,000 to the new seminary.[4] These joined with Morse in founding Andover Theological Seminary.

The purpose of the new seminary, as stated in its constitution, was to increase the "number of learned and able defenders of the Gospel of Christ as well as of orthodox, pious and zealous ministers of the New Testament."[5] The faculty included Edward Dorr Griffen serving as president; Leonard Woods as the Abbot Professor of Christian Theology; Samuel Worcester and Samuel Spring, these latter two representing the Hopkinsians. Each was college educated and a member of either a Presbyterian or a Congregational church.[6]

The entering class of thirty-six students included Adoniram Judson and Gordon Hall. They were joined the following year by Samuel Mills and James Richards. These young men became the core of those vitally concerned with the cause of foreign missions. Andover Theological Seminary made a conscious effort to attract poor but pious youth who would have no other access to the ministry. Candidates for entry were required to have certification of good character and have completed a liberal education including the ability to use Latin and Greek. The school provided them with an education of sound Calvinist principles, room, board and books. In this way the founders hoped to train orthodox ministers to serve throughout the nation. During the early nineteenth century, Andover supplied the majority of pastors for the Congregational churches of Massachusetts, nearly all the missionaries serving the American Board, and many of the Presbyterian ministers serving in the middle and western states. The Reverends

Hiram Bingham, Asa Thurston and William Richards were products of an Andover education.

Another institution of importance for the development of missionary interest and the training of missionaries was the Foreign Missionary School located at Cornwall in Litchfield County, Connecticut. At a meeting at Timothy Dwight's home the founders, John Treadwell, Timothy Dwight, James Morris, Reverend Chapin, Lyman Beecher, Charles Prentice and Joseph Harvey, drew up the constitution for the school. The stated purpose of the institution was "the education . . . of heathen youths, in such a manner, as, with subsequent professional instruction, will qualify them to become useful missionaries, physicians, surgeons, schoolmasters or interpreters, and to communicate to the heathen natives such knowledge of agriculture and the arts, as may prove the means of promoting Christianity and civilization." According to the Panoplist, the students would be taught English, spelling, reading, writing, grammar, arithmetic, geography and religion.[7]

The school not only trained the heathen but also those who hoped to serve as missionaries. Samuel Ruggles, James Ely, Thomas Holman and two of Daniel Chamberlain's sons, Dexter and Nathan, worked at Cornwall before embarking for the Sandwich Islands. The student body included some illustrious students. The impetus for its founding had been the presence of five youths from the Sandwich Islands, one of whom was Henry Opukahaia, or "Obookiah" as he was known in New England.

The young Hawaiians were the best known students at the school in Cornwall. They were first brought to the public's attention by the publication of a pamphlet by the American Board entitled <u>Narrative of Five Youths of the Sandwich Islands</u>. Four of them had been recommended to the American Board and were being taught under Board auspices. These had demonstrated signs of piety. The fifth was under no such conviction, but was the son of the king of Kaua'i, one of the Sandwich Islands. Thomas Hopu [Hopoo] left Hawai'i in 1809, sailing aboard the <u>Triumph</u> with a Captain Brintnell to New Haven. After fighting in the War of 1812, Hopu returned to Connecticut, was converted at Torringford in 1815 and baptized two years later. The <u>Panoplist</u> praised Hopu's known zeal, saying he burned "with ardent desire to carry the heathen glad tidings of salvation to his perishing brethren."[8] John Honoli'i [Honooree] arrived in New England in 1815 and within a year Hopu had assisted his Hawaiian brother in a growing awareness of sin. William Kanu'i [Tennooe] also showed hopeful signs of conversion and was assisted in his quest by a circle of pious females who met weekly to pray for William's conversion. Their prayers were answered at New Haven in 1815. More compelling was the case of George Kaumuali'i [Tamaree] whose father had sent him to America at the age of six. George also served in the War of 1812 and was in the navy when the American Board arranged for him to attend school at Cornwall. George never converted, but in 1818 the <u>Panoplist</u> could assure its readers that George had "seasons of religious impressions."[9]

These four youths gave flesh to the idea of foreign mission, but their presence in New England was eclipsed by that of their fellow Hawaiian, Henry Opukahaia who not only received the grace of a classic conversion experience, but also made the deathbed wish that missionaries be sent to bring God's grace to his countrymen. Opukahaia would become a symbol of foreign missions, not only because of his exemplary life and death but also due to the lives he touched.

Opukahaia had accompanied Thomas Hopu on the journey to New Haven. At first both boys stayed with Captain Brintnell's family. Then, Opukahaia met Timothy Dwight on one of his visits to nearby Yale College and joined his family. In 1810 Opukahaia moved on to Torringford, Connecticut where he stayed with Reverend Samuel Mills, Sr., and studied with Mill's son, Jeremiah. In 1811 Opukahaia journeyed to Andover where he stayed with Samuel Mills, Jr., then to the Bradford Academy at Litchfield where both Lucy Goodale Thurston and Elizabeth Edwards Bishop were educated. Here he boarded with Deacon Hasseltine whose daughter, Anne, later married Adoniram Judson, one of the first missionaries to India. The following year found Opukahaia in Hollis, New Hampshire, where he became ill for five weeks. About the same time the young Hawaiian was touched by the Holy Spirit. "Now the decisive proof of true conversion began to appear."[10]

Opukahaia spent the winter of 1813 with James Morris at Litchfield. That same year Opukahaia requested that his friend, Edwin Dwight, who was preparing for the ministry, serve in Hawai'i. When Dwight did not immediately respond, Opukahaia quoted Matthew 6:25 to him.[11]

In the fall of 1814 Opukahaia appealed to the North Consociation of Litchfield County to be responsible for him. He went back to Torringford and was baptized there in 1816 at the age of twenty-four. "Mr. Mills observes, that the account of [Opkuhaia's] Christian experience . . . was highly satisfactory."[12]

About 1815 the American Board took charge of Opukahaia and the other Hawaiian youths and placed them with their Foreign Mission School at Cornwall. Opukahaia went on a speaking tour with the Reverend Nathan Perkins, an agent of the American Board, to raise funds for the school. Not only were funds raised, but Perkins reported that Opukahaia did a great service for the missionary cause by demonstrating that people of color were not too ignorant to be taught. "The proof [Opukahaia] gave of talents as well as piety, carried conviction to many that the heathen had souls as well as we, and were capable of being enlightened and christianized."[13] Opukahaia continued to speak to people of his love for God and desire to bring the Christian message to Hawai'i. After his speaking tour, Opukahaia was at Andover for two years. He returned to the school at Litchfield in 1817 where he and Samuel Ruggles became close friends. Ruggles resolved that he would accompany Opukahaia home and work with him in the mission field. They both went to Cornwall in 1817.

There Opukahaia was suddenly struck by typhus fever and died on February 17, 1818. The young Hawaiian died with his friends around him in a spirit of cheerful resignation. "I have no desire to live, if I can enjoy the presence of God, and go where Christ is."[14] Opukahaia's only regret was that he was not permitted to evangelize the Hawaiians. Lyman Beecher preached Opukahaia's funeral sermon at the Litchfield Congregational Church, stressing that here was an occasion for a new commitment to the cause of foreign missions. Edwin Dwight, close friend of the deceased, published an edition of Memoirs of Henry Obookiah. It was a runaway bestseller, going through fifty thousand copies in twelve editions with the proceeds going to the American Board. In September 1819 as plans were being made to send the pioneer company of missionaries to Hawaii, the editors of the Panoplist assured their readers that although Opukahaia was dead, "his prayers and supplications with many tears, for his 'poor friends, and relatives and countrymen'. . . will not be forgotten in heaven; nor must they be forgotten on earth."[15] And, they said, the four remaining Hawaiian youths were just as zealous in the cause of mission as their fallen comrade.

Opukahaia did more for the cause of missions in death than he ever had in life. Here was a challenge as necessary and romantic as anything David Brainerd had faced. Hiram Bingham, who never met Opukahaia, but was greatly influenced by him, later reflected in his memoirs that, "Great as were the disappointments and grief at [Opukahaia's] departure, there were consolations in the reflection that the dear youth had himself been plucked as a brand from the burning, and made a trophy of redeeming mercy; and in the hope of his timely conversion, his missionary zeal, his brief and consistent Christian life, and his affecting death, would fan the missionary spirit and hasten the promulgation of the Gospel on the shores that gave him birth." Lucy Thurston and Charles Stewart both agreed that this young man's death had done more for the Hawaiians than a long life of devoted labor ever could have accomplished, because in death Opukahaia was able to arouse the church to send a mission to the Sandwich Islands.[16]

There remains one other key figure for the development of the foreign missionary cause, a young man of a similar character as David Brainerd, or so it seemed to his contemporaries, Samuel Mills, Jr. Young Mills' father, Samuel Mills, Sr., was pastor of the church at Torringford in Litchfield County, Connecticut. In 1798 young Mills was convicted by a revival at Torringford. Though three of Mills' relatives joined the church then, Mills, himself, did not experience conversion until 1801. The senior Mills had been a trustee for the Missionary Society of Connecticut. In 1806, as young Mills entered Williams College, his father embarked on a brief mission to Vermont.

When Mills arrived at Williams College, the school was experiencing a revival. As a part of the revival Mills and several others met for prayer on Wednesdays and Saturdays. One day in August, only five arrived for the prayer meeting; Samuel Mills, James Richards, Francis Robbins, Harvey Loomis and Byron Green. The talk turned to the idea of foreign mission. Mills had been committed to the cause since his conversion. Only Loomis demurred. By 1808 these young men, along with John Nelson, Calvin Bushnell, Rufus Pomeroy, Samuel Ware, Edwin Dwight and Ezra Fisk, had formalized their association into the secret Society of Brethren. Fisk later revealed that the precaution of secrecy was due to the members' modesty. Great care was taken in the selection of members. "No person shall be admitted who is under any engagement of any kind which shall be

incompatible with going on a mission to the heathen."[17]
Activities of the group included the circulation of
sermons on the subject of missions in an effort to
persuade others to support their cause.

After graduation in 1809 the Brethren scattered to
take the call elsewhere. Mills enrolled at Yale, but
found the students unresponsive, and, therefore,
transferred to Andover. While at Yale, Mills
encountered Opukahaia and was appointed his guardian.
The Hawaiian youth made a deep impression on Mills.
Writing his friend, Gordon Hall, about Opukahaia, Mills
speculated, "shall we not rather consider these South
Sea islands [Hawaii] as a proper place for establishing
a mission . . . . We ought not to look only to the
heathen on our own continent; we ought to direct our
attention to that place where we may . . . do the most
good, and where the difficulties are the least."[18]

The Society of Brethren was re-established at
Andover in 1810; and Adoniram Judson, Samuel Nott and
Samuel Newell became active in the movement. The
Brethren launched a public organization, the Society of
Inquiry on the Subject of Missions, in 1811 open to any
student who had been at Andover three months and showed
signs of piety and affection for missionary activity.
This group would work out the best method of conducting
a mission and inquire into the state of unbelievers.

Mills believed there were sound reasons why the
time was ripe for foreign missions. American churches
were wealthy and that wealth should be spent spreading
the gospel; no one could still plead ignorance
concerning the foreign unbelievers, and there were other
organizations caring for the home mission field. Great

Britain was leading the way to missionary success, but Americans should sponsor their own enterprise. When Judson considered offering his services to the London Missionary Society, Mills responded, "What! is England to support her own missionaries and ours as well . . . I do not like this dependence upon another nation, especially when they have done so much, and we nothing."[19]

II

It was Samuel Mills, Jr. and the fellow members of the Society of Brethren at Andover Theological Seminary who made the object of foreign missions a reality. First the society met with sympathetic professors. Then, with official support, the students presented the Bradford Memorial to the General Association meeting of Massachusetts in 1810. The Brethren asserted that if there was no American organization to sponsor them, they would join the London Missionary Society. They need not have worried. The American Board of Commissioners for Foreign Missions was organized under Calvinist ecumenical auspices on June 29, 1810. Five members were from Massachusetts and four from Connecticut. Their first task was to arouse public interest in the cause and support of foreign missions through the Panoplist and other appropriate publications as well as speaking tours and sermons.

The task was to draw attention to the plight of unbelievers. In May 1810, the Panoplist urged its readers to "go to your closet; fall on your knees; and, if never before, pray for the poor heathen. Pray for the few, who have left all to carry them the news of a Savior. Pray that more missionaries may be sent forth.

And whenever you have a view of Jesus, and have been weeping over the scene of his dying love; whenever your souls are melted into pious tenderness and turned to heavenly joys, Oh, forget not to pray for the poor heathen." Prayer would not be enough, but it was a beginning. Four months later readers were informed that their prayers were answered. Several young men of pious reputation were ready to spread the gospel anywhere in the world. Yet, they needed public support. "Shall this support be wanting? When millions are perishing for lack of knowledge, and young disciples of the Lord are waiting . . . to carry the gospel of salvation to them."[20]

The answer was no, the unbelievers would not perish for want of public support. In 1812 the first missionary enterprise of the American Board embarked for India. Adoniram Judson, Samuel Newell, Gordon Hall, Samuel Nott and Luther Rice together with their wives began the great adventure. At their ordination sermon, Leonard Woods observed, "Christians have wanted some grand object to seize their hearts and engage all their powers . . . . The spread of the gospel and the conversion of the world constitute the very object wanted, -- the common cause which ought to unite . . . the great family of christians."[21]

Christian unity suffered a setback, however, when Judson and Rice converted to the Baptist theology on the voyage to India. But that apostasy was soon overshadowed by the sentimental memoirs of Charlotte Newell who died shortly after her arrival in the mission field and the excitement of launching a mission to Ceylon (Sri Lanka) in 1814. Letters from Bombay convinced the American Board and friends of mission that "the missionary work is great, painful and arduous, and requires primitive self-devotion, invincible perseverance and bounteous liberality; but they made it appear that if the work be conducted with the true spirit, in the right manner, and with adequate means, accompanied with the promised influence and blessing of Heaven, the Gospel . . . may spread through the heathen world."[22]

Unfortunately, by 1816 contributions to the American Board had declined. There were several reasons including the postwar recession, the Baptist apostasy and the fact that India and Ceylon (Sri Lanka) were too remote to hold public interest. The American Board sponsored the Foreign Mission School as a means of keeping the public focus on mission. That focus was intensified with the death of Opukahaia, an unbeliever who had received Christ. "Shall the holy flame be quenched?" queried Samuel Worcester, secretary of the American Board's Prudential Committee, "Shall these dear young disciples [from Hawai'i] not be allowed and encouraged to return, and publish in their native Isles the Good Tidings . . . . Shall they be sent back alone, -- without means -- without aid?" The Sandwich Islands were ripe "for Christian charity and Christian hope . . . kindly disposed, desirous of civilization."[23] The Sandwich Islands were exotic, but also had the familiarity of whaler and shipping contacts since the 1780s. They were foreign, but not under British control. The people were ignorant, but able to learn. The public enthusiasm for the Sandwich Islands field is reflected in the hymn William B. Tappan, a noted

philanthropist, composed for the departure of the Second
Company embarking for that destination.   It was an
enthusiasm which the fields in Asia, the Middle East and
among the American Indians could not match.

> Wake, Isles of the South! Your redemption is near
> No longer repose in the borders of gloom;
> The strength of his chosen in love will appear,
> And light shall arise on the verge of the tomb,
> Alleluia to the Lamb who hath purchased our pardon;
> We will praise again when we pass over Jordan.
>
> The billows that girt ye, the wild waves that roar,
> The zephyrs that play where the ocean storms cease,
> Shall bear the rich freight to your desolate shore,
> Shall waft glad tidings of pardon and peace,
> Alleluia . . .
>
> On islands that sit in the regions of night,
> The lands of despair, to oblivion a prey;
> The morning will open with healing and light
> The young star of Bethlehem will ripen to-day
> Alleluia . . .
>
> The altar and idol in dust overthrown,
> The incense forbade that was hallowed in blood;
> The priest of Melehisedee there shall atone,
> And shrines of Attooi be sacred to God!
> Alleluia . . .
>
> The heathen will hasten to welcome the time,
> The day-spring, the prophet, in vision once saw --
> When the beams of Messiah will illumine each clime
> And isles of the ocean shall wait for his law.
> Alleluia . . .
>
> And thou OBOOKIAH! now sainted above,
> Will rejoice as the heralds of mission disclose;
> And the prayer will be heard, that the land thou didst love,
>
> May blossom as Sharon, and bud as the rose!
> Alleluia . . .[24]

III

Despite the dedication of men like Samuel Mills,
and the inspiration of Opukahaia, there remained the

problem of defining what was entailed in a foreign mission and who should embark upon such an enterprise. In this regard, Americans looked to their British brethren for initial guidance due to that nation's experience with the problem.

David Bogue's <u>Objections Against a Mission to the Heathen</u>, <u>Stated and Considered</u> was a popular source, mentioned by both Levi Chamberlain and Charles Stewart as material the Second Company gave particular attention to during the voyage to the Sandwich Islands. Bogue's thoughts had first been presented as a sermon to the founders of the London Missionary Society in 1795. The sermon was reprinted by the Society of Inquiry on the Subject of Missions at Andover Theological Seminary, perhaps as late as 1811.

Bogue proclaimed from the outset that the propagation of the gospel was a duty. "[Christ] has taught us the strong obligations we are to pity those who are sitting in darkness and in the shadow of death." The Apostle Paul did not ignore the idolatrous Athenians and Bogue's contemporaries could not ignore the idolatrous heathen.[25]

As to the qualities of a missionary, Bogue asserted that "did we but view a missionary as we ought, and as he is, with Jesus . . . at his right hand . . . and the Holy Spirit resting on him like a flame of fire, with all his powerful energies" then we would maintain hope in the face of pagan ignorance. "The rays of divine knowledge must shine forth brightly from [the missionary's] mind" and "to the light of knowledge there must be added, in a good missionary, the celestial heat of zeal; pure, ardent, persevering zeal for the glory of

God, and the salvation of man, must, like unextinguished
fire upon the altar, burn continually within his breast,
unabated by all the difficulties and discouragements."
Bogue went on to state that a missionary must also add
"the wisdom of the serpent to the harmlessness of the
dove, the most exalted devotion, the most profound
humility, unconquerable meekness, and patience under
sufferings and trials." The reason for this zeal and
perseverance could only be active benevolence for it
"teaches us to do good, both to the bodies and souls of
men."[26] Bogue's exhortations had an Edwardsean flavor,
and both consistent and orthodox American Calvinists
approved of them; the theme was enlarged but never
replaced.

A month before the formal organization of the
American Board in May 1810, the Panoplist expressed
"Concern for the Salvation of the Heathen." Christ had
issued the Great Commission, yet Christians allowed
"three fourths of the world [to] sleep the sleep of
death." The article pleaded that "young men, whose
souls are fired with divine love, forsake your friends
and native land. Forsake all for Christ. Go into the
destitute regions of the earth and spend your days in
winning souls."[27]

Seven months later the Panoplist reprinted an
article from the London Missionary Society discussing
the motives of missionary candidates. "It is only a
sincere, deep, and steady love to Christ, and a desire
to promote his kingdom among men, even at the hazard of
your life, and at the sacrifice of worldly ease and
interest, which can form the foundation of the true
Missionary character." The article said to the

prospective candidate: "Do you then desire to engage in this work, from a conviction that it is your duty to devote yourself therein to the service of God? that it is the most beneficial way of employing your existence? that it is your highest wisdom to be thus consecrated to his glory? and that this is the most suitable expression of your gratitude to him?" If the candidate could answer yes to these questions, he or she would probably make a good missionary. However, the article urged the candidate to consider the choice carefully. "He who puts his hand to the Missionary plough ought not to look back."[28] Duty, benevolence, sacrifice, loneliness, danger, love of God, gratitude to Christ, and rescuing ignorant heathen; these were the constant themes of the literature on foreign mission. Mission was the great selfless act. But who would be called? How would the candidates experience the call?

Upon arrival in the mission field of Hawai'i, Clarissa Lyman Richards recalled, "While in America my imagination had often portrayed scenes of the future -- The humble cot on missionary ground, and all its appurtenances fancy had dressed in fairy colours -- She had twined around her happy dwelling many romantic sweets, and scattered with a lavish hand the beauties of natural scenery. You will ask if the picture exists in real life. I answer no."[29] What were the expectations of missionary life which the evangelists to Hawai'i cherished before their arrival in the mission field brought them face to face with reality?

Sybil Mosely Bingham first mentioned a call to foreign mission on September 12, 1818. She had attended a meeting where she "heard the call of perishing millions" and responded, "gladly do I seek my chamber feeling that I would shut my eyes, my ears, my heart to this vain world." Sybil Mosely struggled with her decision. In December she wrote that her "hesitancy did not arise from a less willingness to pass my short life among the heathen, but from this, whether it were a sacrifice to which God called me." She left the matter with God. Less than a year later, enroute to the Sandwich Islands, she exclaimed, "I am filled with astonishment that thus thou shouldst honor me, by giving me the prospect of labouring and suffering for thee. . . in a revolted province of thy dominions." Upon further consideration, Sybil Bingham exulted, "I have felt that the advancement of Christ's kingdom was an object which weighed down every personal consideration. There have been times within the few past years, when I have found it good to seek my closet and ask GOD to send me to the heathen; - to-night I feel that I would bless his name that he has brought me thus far on my way to them; 'tho it be to suffer yea, I think to die."[30] If she could have seen into the future, young Mrs. Bingham would undoubtedly have been disappointed to learn that after twenty-one years in the field, her death would be an anticlimactic one in Easthampton, Massachusetts.

Mercy Partridge Whitney was less effusive. Writing her cousin, Josiah Brewer, on February 4, 1819, Mercy Partridge commented that she had been perusing a history of missions by one Mr. Lord. "I think it well calculated to inspire a missionary spirit. I at times almost fancy myself with the dear brethren, sharing their trials, and with them encountering the difficulties and hardships of missionary life." Brewer seems to have taken his cousin's comments seriously, and found her a suitor of the same bent. In a letter of August 30, Mercy Partridge agreed that Brewer's friend could visit her, but "the subject to which you have directed my thoughts is of infinite moment . . . . For several years past I have felt an earnest desire for the salvation of my fellow men, but more particularly the poor heathen who are groping in pagan darkness." Mercy Partridge was not "insensible that the sacrifices which I must make are very great, but when I consider what Christ has done for me a worthless worm of dust, can I refuse?"[31]

One has the feeling that Mercy Partridge is less than excited about the mission field, that it is not the destination of choice, but of duty. Writing to her brother, William Partridge, and his wife, Laura, the next month, Mercy explained, "If you have experienced the love of God . . . and have felt the worth of an immortal soul, the awful condition of man by nature, the lamentable state of the heathen world, & the need of missionary labours; I think you will not brand me with enthusiasm when I tell you that I expect soon to engage in a mission." It is clear from Mercy Whitney's journal that though she is effusive in her piety and fervent in her concern for the souls of friends and family, the role of assistant missionary was not a comfortable one. Enroute to her station, the young woman confessed, "were I assured that this is the path selected for me by my Heavenly Father, I would rejoice in the midst of trials and privations. This consolation I for the most part enjoy. But at times, when I reflect upon the magnitude

of the missionary work and my unfitness for it, I am led
to doubt respecting the path of duty."[32]

Lucy Goodale Thurston made her choice with quiet
logic. "The poor heathen possess immortal natures and
are perishing. Who will give them the Bible and tell
them of a Savior?" Once the decision was made,
Mrs. Thurston "could contemplate the subject with a
tranquil mind and unmoved feelings."[33] Maria Sartwell
Loomis was of the same opinion. After an emotional
departure, she commented, "I still think it an honor &
a privilege to engage in the great work of evangelizing
the Heathen."[34]

Martha Barnes Goodrich reflected most eloquently
the mixed emotions of her missionary sisters. Sailing
aboard the _Thames_, Mrs. Goodrich felt "confident that if
my heavenly Father has anything for me to do in those
pagan Isles, he will carry me safely there, and enable
me to accomplish it. And if he has nothing for me to do
there, nor anywhere else, I know not why I should wish
to live." Mrs. Goodrich understood that her call to the
missionary field was not an easy one. "I must be
prepared for disappointment. A missionary life will .
. . be peculiarly exposed to them, trouble and sorrow
will in all probability attend my future life, and
perhaps the only . . . consolation I shall have, will be
the thought that I am walking in the path of duty."
Yet, in spite of her apprehension, Martha Goodrich
rejoiced to be part of the mission, that her parents had
been so willing to part with her and that no obstacles
had been placed in her path. Mrs. Goodrich believed her
hardships would be as nothing compared to what Christ
had done for her.[35]

Martha Goodrich's relief that her parents had not placed obstacles in her path was real, for several of the missionaries met opposition to their call from friends and family. "I can find no such place in scripture that it is the duty of females to go," wrote an exasperated cousin, S. Howe, to Elizabeth Edwards. "I think you may do as much good here as you possibly could go to the islands of the seas."[36] One of the missionary sisters, Harriet Tiffany Stewart, in effect, ran away with her husband. Sarah Shepherd, Hiram Bingham's first choice as a bride, refused the missionary's suit because her parents would not allow her to make such a sacrifice. Bingham would later comment that "while thousands treated the self-immolation of the missionaries . . . as truly commendable, tens of thousands regarded it as foolish or fanatical or an uncalled for sacrifice of comfort, property, and life. By many, the missionaries were urged to a different course, because there was so much to be done at home, or because it would cost so much to complete the plan abroad, or because they did not think it of much importance that the heathen should ever hear the Gospel. Nearly all the early missionaries . . . were strenuously opposed by their parents, relatives and friends."[37]

Indeed, Charles Stewart commented with some puzzlement on the general public's astonishment that any sane person would embark on a foreign mission. As the Thames passed uninhabited Staten Island where some sailors had been left to catch seals, Stewart mused, "I could not help but wonder at the inconsistency of those who condemn the Missionary to a heathen land as an enthusiast and a mad man, and yet look on such as these, who, for a little worldly gain, banish themselves for months and years to the most inhospitable climes, as praiseworthy examples of enterprise and hardihood."[38]

The question of a missionary's function was particularly acute for the women, whom the American Board classified as assistant missionaries, a seeming misnomer for women who went through such anguish to determine their respective missionary calls. Yet, in all probability, these women were less concerned with their title than their vocation, especially since only ordained ministers received the ultimate distinction of being titled "missionary."

There was some discussion as to whether women should be sent into the company of the heathen, and the American Board denied them access to some stations, such as the Middle East. In the early years, no single woman could apply, a decision with which Martha Goodrich concurred. "I should never advise a female to go alone on a foreign mission. An unmarried female must be placed in a very unpleasant situation on board a ship especially to go so long a voyage. There are many reasons why I would not be in such a situationon any account."[39] Once again, the American Board was guided by their more experienced English brethren. George Bruder of the London Missionary Society recommended that those chosen to be missionary wives must be "truly pious persons, of tried integrity and unblemished character; prudent, domestic, humble; not looking for great things in this world."[40]

At first women seemed to have a glorious purpose as missionaries. Reverend Jonathan Allen charged those women embarking for India in 1812 "to teach these [heathen] women, to whom your husbands have but little or no access. Go then, and do all in your power, to enlighten their minds, and bring them to the knowledge of the truth. Go . . . raise their character to the dignity of rational beings, and to the rank of Christians . . . . Teach them to realize, that they are not an inferior race . . . but stand on a par with men. Teach them that they have immortal souls."[41] Such a prospect could excite a young woman's idealism and religious zeal. It was also in keeping with the slowly emerging belief that women were the keepers of the religious flame. Samuel Ruggles, writing his sister, Lucia, to encourage her interest in the Sandwich Islands mission, pointed out that her "sex in general [was] much more forward in the pious work of diffusing spiritual knowledge among the heathen than the male." Ruggles offered no proof of this except to say that women "have ever shown much greater attachment to the Saviour than men."[42] The latter was a fact often commented upon during revivals.

The situation changed after 1812. Charlotte Newell had perished upon arrival in the Asian mission field. The American Board had a greater sense of the hardship of missionary life. Yet, the Board defended its decision to send women to the Sandwich Islands. "It was not in regard to things merely temporal that Woman was designed." Nor was there any law of heaven to exclude them from "recovering the common race, lost in consequence of her being deceived who was first in the transgression." Women would help the brethren by their "assiduous attentions, their affectionate offices, their prudent suggestions, their cheering influences [and] their unceasing prayers." Women would also show the islanders "an effective example of the purity, and dignity, and lovliness [sic] . . . the attractive and celestial excellence, which Christianity can impart to the Female Character."[43]

Artemas Bishop, writing from the field, had a more succinct appraisal. "A missionary ought not to live here without a wife." In the Sandwich Islands a woman "need never be at a loss for business. Besides contributing to the comfort, respectability & usefulness of her husband, and superintending her family concerns, she will find ample employment in instructing the natives, especially the females, in reading, writing & sewing."[44] Indeed, Bishop's assessment was a true job description for the female missionary. Writing in her journal, Sybil Bingham would despair that she had so little time to study the Hawaiian language and/or the Bible. "You may wonder, sometimes, what, in this corner of the earth, I can find to be doing, if it be not laboring for the heathen."[45] Levi Chamberlain did not wonder. Chamberlain informed the American Board that he was "satisfied that most of the ladies . . .have too much domestic care."[46]

Men contemplated the idea of missionary work with much the same mixture of emotions as the women. Though their testimony is less sentimental the realization of duty and the allure of romance and adventure are evident. Asa Thurston writing the American Board of his fitness for the missionary call stated that when asked who would go to the heathen, he could only reply, "here am I Lord, send me." But he also wrote, "Often have I in imagination sat down by the cottage of the wretched pagan & endeavoured to instruct him in the principles of our holy religion . . . . I have often seemed to see the tear start from his eye as I pointed him to 'the love of Jesus.'" Thurston was aware that "these things may appear to be the result of a <u>vagrant</u> imagination, but I have taken much pleasure in such thoughts arising, in part perhaps, from the expectation, that I might hereafter be conversant with such scenes." Thurston may have waxed sentimental over his potential spiritual charges, but he reassured the Board that he did not take such a vocation lightly. It was necessary that some people must serve unbelievers and that they do so from a conviction of personal duty.[47] Thurston took those duties seriously, serving the remainder of his life in Hawai'i.

William Richards was not unacquainted with the requirements of the missionary life. His brother, James, served with he American Board's mission in Asia. Richards declared that, "With a view to self-examination I sometimes change [places] with my brother and there found myself in sickly body in a heathen land," but, he exclaimed, "the prospect of a man's death . . . does not discourage me."[48]

Elisha Loomis seems almost attracted by the thought of such a romantic death. "What glorious achievement was ever moved without danger?" he asked, "What if I meet with death! Could I desire to die in a more glorious way?" Indeed, he was only doing "what I feel persuaded is my <u>duty</u>: and am doing it cheerfully."[49] Loomis' conversion led him to renounce the world. Soon after Loomis found his compassion "excited at the relation of cruel practices and horrid rites of the heathen nations; and tears of sympathy often stole down my cheeks while reading of the widow burnt on the funeral pile and the poor pilgrim crushed by the wheels of the bloody Juggernaut. I viewed with pleasure the numberless efforts making to meliorate the condition of the wretched."[50] It would seem apparent that Mr. Loomis was a regular reader of the Panoplist.

Artemas Bishop took a more solemn view. "I have ever viewed the office of a Missionary of Jesus as one of self-denial -- as attended with much perplexity and disappointment, & which is by no means free from peril. Still I have & do consider it as the highest & noblest undertaking ever apprised by man."[51]

The decision to become a missionary had not been made lightly. Bishop was affected by Samuel Newell's death in India and in 1821 wrote his sister, Eliza, "the impression has been on my mind for more than 2 years, that it would be my duty to go on a foreign mission." The missionary candidate took special precautions to ensure that his call to mission was from God. "If after having inquired into my qualifications for a missionary life, for 2 or 3 years -- if after having made it the burden of my prayer to God for a long time to give me direction -- if after feeling that in no other situation I should be in the path of duty -- If after all this I think it my duty to go, I think it will amount to a call."[52]

Daniel Chamberlain was unusual among his fellow missionaries. He was not a young man, but a prosperous farmer, married, the father of five. yet, his response was the same as his younger co-workers. Writing from the mission field, Chamberlain remembered that for some years before leaving America, he "had an ardent desire to labor for Christ among the heathen -- My mind was much occupied with the subject -- I often lamented that I had neglected while young to acquire and education . . . . But the circumstance of my being settled in life with a family of small children seemed to forbid the hope."[53]   As to Chamberlain's decision to uproot his family and take them into the "wilderness," Eliakin Phelps observed there could be no other motivation than the "desire to do good."[54] Chamberlain responded to his selection with humility and a trust in God. He was at peace in Hawai'i commenting, "I have no wish to exchange my calling for any on earth."[55]

Levi Chamberlain entertained no doubts but several frustrations regarding foreign missions. In 1826 Levi Chamberlain wrote his brother, Joseph, of his realization of the need for missions. "I clearly saw that all men of all nations, of every land and every language, stood in like need of the Gospel . . . . With these convictions, I felt it my duty to leave my native land and go to the heathen." In September 1821 Levi Chamberlain requested that the American Board employ him as a teacher among the Indians. Instead, he was appointed secretary to Samuel Worcester. Though his services in this capacity were of real use to the cause of missions, Levi was frustrated with the position. "I have thought Providence had been disciplining me by a series of trials, by sickness, by teaching me how to abound & in some small degree to suffer need for a service requiring self [denial] & possibly suffering," he wrote to Jeremiah Evarts, "God only knows the occult

motive of my Soul; but I do not feel fully reconciled to
the idea of giving up all expectation of going as an
assistant missionary to the heathen."[56]   In 1822 the
American Board finally sent Chamberlain to Hawai'i as
the secular agent for the mission.

Hiram Bingham, perhaps the best known of the
missionaries to Hawai'i, had much to write on the
subject of his missionary call. Bingham's brother, the
Reverend Amos Bingham, had brought the missionary cause
to Bingham's attention before he entered Andover
Theological Seminary.   Bingham struggled with the
problem for six years. Writing his parents in February
1819, Bingham declared, "I love my friends --I love my
country -- I love the church at home," yet, he
concluded, "these very blessings bestowed on me make it
my duty to impart them to others . . . . For the
opportunity to 'do good' confers the obligation to 'do
good.'" The deaths of Henry Opukahaia and Samuel Mills,
Jr. greatly affected Bingham. Writing Samuel Worcester,
Bingham confided that on a visit to Cornwall he was
deeply touched "when I saw those dear youth whom God .
. . had brought from pagan lands." Young Bingham seemed
to hear God say, "Who will go for us -- [Opukahaia] is
dead -- his lamented benefactor is dead . . . . other
laborers are ready to press into that field -- but no
educated missionary has yet volunteered."   Bingham
responded to the call.   "Finding nothing in the
circumstances of my own case, as to health, friends,
engagements, or the prospect of patronage & success
which would excuse me from going to the heathen," he
concluded that all would be best served if he accepted
the call.[57]

IV

Betsey Stockton also received a call to mission, however, her inclusion in the Second Company (1823) of American Board missionaries to Hawai'i was highly irregular. Betsey Stockton was the only black American associated with the Sandwich Islands Mission. Although subjected to the same admission procedures as the other candidates, and officially assigned to the position of teacher, Miss Stockton's position was tied to the Stewart household, and her acceptance had much to do with the poor health of Mrs. Harriet Stewart.[58]

Miss Stockton was a freed slave, working as a domestic servant for her former owner, the Reverend Ashbel Green. Reverend Green was instrumental in the Reverend Charles Stewart's acceptance of the missionary call. Presumably Green did not want Stewart's services precluded by Mrs. Stewart's poor health, and was the intermediary between the Stewarts and Miss Stockton.

For her part, Betsey Stockton was a member of the First Presbyterian Church at Princeton, New Jersey and had expressed a desire to serve as a missionary to Africa. Since such a mission was not feasible, Miss Stockton apparently concluded she could best serve the cause of missions by assisting the Stewarts and working in the Sandwich Islands as a teacher.

Although the association of the Stewarts and the American Board required that of Miss Stockton, her membership in the Second Company placed the Board in a peculiar position. The American Board hoped to increase its fundraising efforts in the southern and western United States, the very areas which would be most offended by the thought of black missionaries. Hence,

the American Board made every effort to downplay Betsey
Stockton's presence in the Second Company. Newspaper
coverage of the __Thames__' departure, for example,
published lists of the missionaries and their helpers.
Betsey Stockton's name came after those of the Hawaiian
and Tahitian helpers.[59] Betsey Stockton's journals and
letters were given little publicity and appeared
primarily in the __Christian Advocate__ published by her
former owner, the Reverend Ashbel Green.

The unusual circumstances surrounding Betsey
Stockton's addition to the Second Company led to the
ratification of the unique document printed below. Its
purpose was to specify Miss Stockton's relationship to
the American Board, the Stewarts, and the mission family
as a whole. Miss Stockton was to occupy a position
greater than a servant, but less than an equal. She was
to relieve Mrs. Stewart of her domestic concerns, and
serve the mission as a teacher.

The Stewarts took great pains to treat Miss
Stockton as an equal,[60] but other members of the mission
family perceived her as a member of the Stewart
household and treated her with the relative indifference
due a domestic servant. In fact, without the written
document, her position might well have been untenable.
Dr. Abraham Blatchely, in particular, was open in his
regard of Miss Stockton's servile station. The doctor
was concerned that the Hawaiian climate in conjunction
with the hardship of domestic labor not only exhausted
missionary wives, but forced husbands to take time from
their duties to assist the women. Blatchely complained
that the Stewarts' "colored girl" would be useful in

this regard, but the Stewarts would not share her services.[61]

Blatchely also wanted to use Miss Stockton's services as a nurse, but the Stewarts replied that they would nurse the sick themselves before allowing her to do so. "No one here," sniffed Dr. Blatchely, "can suppose from appearances that [the Stewarts] ever design to attend as Nurse on their Brethren or Sisters."[62] And, in fact, Miss Stockton found that teaching her Hawaiian pupils and caring for the Stewarts occupied all her time.

Life in the mission field proved to be very lonely for Miss Stockton. She shared her sense of isolation and spiritual doubt with Levi Chamberlain, the only other unmarried missionary. "I have indeed found that it is an evil and bitter thing to depart from the living God, my want of faith and my constant inclination to sin . . . it was then that I felt the want of some Christian friend in whom I could confide."[63]

Levi Chamberlain eventually married and remained in the field; Miss Stockton did neither. Even with assistance, Mrs. Stewart was unable to cope with the Hawaiian climate, and the entire household returned to the United States in October 1825.

The document printed below defined the relationship of Betsey Stockton and her employers, the American Board of Commissioners for Foreign Missions.[64] Its purpose was to prevent her exploitation; its very existence reveals much about the social realities of early nineteenth century America.

> Betsey Stockton, a colored young woman brought up in the family of the Rev. Ashbel Green, having been received with the Rev. Charles S. Stewart and his wife, as a missionary to the Sandwich islands by

the American Board of Commissioners for Missions; -- it is thought that it may be useful, as there is something peculiar in her case, to specify in writing the views of the undersigned in regard to her and the part which she is to act in the sacred work in which she is to be engaged.

First.   She is to be considered as, at all times, under the entire direction and control of the American Board of Commissioners for Foreign Missions.

Second.   With the approbation of the Board, she is to be considered in the first instance as specially attached to the family of the Rev. Charles S. Stewart, and as constituting a member of his family.

Third.   In this family, she is to be regarded & treated neither as an equal nor as a servant -- but as an humble christian friend, embarked in the great enterprise of endeavoring to ameliorate the condition of the heathen generally, & especially to bring them to the saving knowledge of the truth as it is in Jesus.

Fourth.   As she is to endeavor to lighten the burden of Mr. and Mrs. Stewart's family care, as much as possible, consistently with her other engagements as a missionary; and especially to relieve Mrs. Stewart in the more laborious parts of domestic concerns.

Fifth.   She is to see in Mr. & Mrs. Stewart her particular friends, patrons, & protectors; -- to look to them for counsel and aid, and to regard their opinions and wishes as the guide of her conduct, so far as these may consist with a supreme regard to the glory and commands of God.

Sixth.   Out of the family of Mr. Stewart, she is to endeavor to render every service to the mission in her power, But not to be called on, as of right, for any menial services, more than any other member of

the mission, as this might manifestly
render her life servile, and prevent her
being employed as a teacher of a school,
for which it is hoped that she will be
found qualified. --

Seventh.   It is understood that if Mr. Stewart
should, at any time, be disposed to
separate Betsey from his family, or if
she should be disposed to leave it, or if
it should be mutually thought desirable
that they should separate -- all the
parties concerned will be a full liberty
to do so -- And in such event, Betsey
will remain under the care and
superintendence of the Board, like any
other missionary.

The undersigned, having mutually and deliberately
considered, and cordially approved the premises,
have subscribed the same at Princeton, New Jersey,
this twenty fourth day of October, in the year of
our Lord One thousand eight hundred & twenty two.

Ashbel Green
Chas. Saml. Stewart,
Betsey Stockton
New Haven, Nov. 18, 1822

Approved in behalf of the American Board of
Commissioners for Foreign Missions by
Jer. Evarts, Cor. Sec. &
Clerk of the Prudential Committee
A true copy, attest

Levi Chamberlain[64]

V

Most of the missionaries arriving in Hawai'i were
young and untried.   All were under the spell of their
theology and the romantic image of missionary life.   And
yet, for the vast majority, their vocation was firm.
Writing his memoirs thirty years later, Bingham cut
through all the uncertainty of youth and the more
romantic aspects of the call, stating simply, "The

object for which the missionaries felt themselves impelled to visit the Hawaiian race, was to honor God . . . and to benefit those heathen tribes, by making them acquainted with the way of life, -- to turn them from their follies and crimes, idolatries and oppressions, to the service and enjoyment of the living God . . . to give them the Bible in their own tongue, with ability to read it for themselves, -- to introduce and extend among them the more useful arts and usages of civilized and Christianized society, and to fill the habitable parts of those important islands with schools and churches, fruitful fields, and pleasant dwellings."[65]

Despite the unexpected reality of the Hawaiian culture and the isolation of individual mission stations, these idealistic Christians persevered. But they also wavered between romanticism and duty; love for the Hawaiians and fear for their own spiritual and temporal lives.

THE MACEDONIAN CALL - ENDNOTES

1. Isaac Davis and John Young were two British seamen who had arrived in Hawai'i aboard the Fair American and Eleanora, respectively. Davis was the sole survivor when the Fair American was attacked at Honuaula, Maui in retaliation for deeds done there by Captain Simon Metcalfe of the Eleanora. Meanwhile, the Eleanora was at anchor in Kealakekua Bay where John Young went ashore and was detained by Kamehameha who feared that if Metcalfe learned what had happened to the Fair American, he would retaliate. Davis and Young became friends; both worked as advisors to Kamehameha I and were treated as ali'i.
Panoplist, October 1808, p. 236.

2. Clarissa Lyman Richards, February 3, 1823, Journal, JC, HMSCL.

3. Charles S. Stewart, Journal, op. cit., pp. 83-84.

4. John Norris offers an interesting example of the network of New England Calvinism. Norris was a wealthy shipowner, a Hopkinsian, and a member of the congregation led by Samuel Hopkins' brother, Daniel. Norris had an interest in missionary work, possibly due to the fortune he had made in India, and was persuaded that the missionary cause would best be served by training ministers. Norris agreed to financially assist the new seminary at Andover, provided that two of the founding professors were Hopkinsians. After Norris' death, his widow gave the American Board $30,000, enabling it to send its first missionaries to India. Figures taken from Elsbree, op. cit., p. 97; see also, Lois Wendland Banner, "The Protestant Crusade: Religious Missions, Benevolence and Reform in the United States, 1790-1840" (Ph.D. dissertation, Columbia University, 1970), pp. 165-166; and DeJong, op. cit., p. 549.

5. William Warren Sweet, Religion in the Development of American Culture, op. cit., p. 678.

6. Presbyterians and Congregationalists established the Plan of Union in 1801 to facilitate missionary efforts, particularly in the home missionary field. Each denomination agreed to recognize the other's ministry and polity. Princeton, a Presbyterian

seminary, also trained ministers who served the American Board, for example, Charles Stewart and Aretmas Bishop.

7. Hiram Bingham, <u>A Residence of Twenty-one Years in the Sandwich Islands</u> (Rutland Vt: Charles E. Tuttle Company, 1981), p. 58; <u>Panoplist</u>, February 1817, pp. 80-81.

8. <u>Panoplist</u>, November 1817, pp. 517-518; Quote: Ibid., November 1818, pp. 512-513.

9. <u>Panoplist</u>, November 1818, pp. 512-513.

10. Edwin Dwight, <u>Memoirs of Henry Obookiah</u> (1818; reprint, Honolulu: Women's Board of Missions for the Pacific Islands, 1968), pp. 31-32.

11. Ibid., pp. 33-34. "Therefore I say unto you, Take no thought for your life, what ye shall eat, or what ye shall drink; nor yet for your body, what ye shall put on. Is not the life more than meat, and the body than raiment?" (Mt. 6:25 KJV)

12. E. Dwight, <u>Narrative of Five Youth from the Sandwich Islands</u> (New York: J. Seymour, 1816), p. 10.

13. Ibid., pp. 74-75.

14. Ibid., p. 95.

15. <u>Panoplist</u>, September 1819, p. 229.

16. Bingham, <u>Residence</u>, p. 59. Lucy G. Thurston, <u>Life and Times</u>, op. cit., p. 2.; Stewart, <u>Journal</u>, pp. 31-32.

17. Thomas C. Richards, <u>Samuel J Mills: Missionary Pathfinder, Pioneer and Promoter</u> (Boston: The Pilgrim Press, 1906), pp. 35-36.

18. Ibid., p. 97.

19. Ibid., pp. 58-59. Rowe, p. 114.

20. <u>Panoplist</u>, May 1810, p. 546; and, September 1811, p. 180; September 1810, p. 126.

21. Leonard Woods, A Sermon, in Pioneers in Mission, ed.
    R. Pierce Beaver (Grand Rapids: B. Eeerdmans
    Publishing Company, 1966), p. 265.

22. Panoplist, April 1816, p. 186.

23. Samuel Worcester, Mission to the Sandwich Islands
    (Boston: U. Crocker, Printer, 1819), pp. 2-3.

24. Panoplist, January 1823, p. 12.

25. David Bogue, Objections Against a Mission to the
    Heathen, Stated and Considered (Cambridge: Hilliard
    and Metcalf, 1811), pp. 7, 12.

26. Ibid., pp. 15-16, 23.

27. Panoplist, May 1810, pp. 545-546.

28. Ibid., December 1810, pp. 336-338.

29. Clarissa Lyman Richards, May 1, 1823, Journal, JC,
    HMCSL.

30. Sybil Moseley Bingham, September 12, 1818, December
    27, 1818, November 8, 1819, February 7, 1820,
    Journal, JC, HMCSL.

31. Mercy Partridge Whitney to Josiah Brewer, February
    4, 1819, August 30, 1819, ML, HMCSL.

32. Mercy Partridge Whitney to William & Laura
    Partridge, September 27, 1829, ML; December 31,
    1819, Journal, JC, HMCSL.

33. Lucy Goodale Thurston, Life and Times op. cit., pp.
    5-6.

34. Elisha & Maria Sartwell Loomis, October 23, 1829,
    Journal, JC, HMCSL.

35. Martha Barnes Goodrich, December 19 & December 23,
    1822, March 15, 1823, Journal (New Haven: Darris &
    Peck, n.d.).

36. S. Howe to Elizabeth Edwards Bishop, September 15,
    1822, ML, HMCSL.

37. Bingham, Residence, op. cit., p. 62.

38. Charles S. Stewart, _Journal_, op. cit., p. 71.

39. M. Goodrich, December 14, 1822, _Journal_.

40. _Panoplist_, September 1811, p. 182.

41. Jonathan Allen, "A Sermon . . . February 5, 1812," in _Pioneers in Mission_, op. cit.

42. Samuel Ruggles to Lucia Ruggles Holman, March 1819, ML, HMCSL.

43. Heman Humphrey, _The Promised Land_ (Boston: Samuel T. Armstrong, 1819), pp. xii-xiii.

44. Artemas Bishop to Jeremiah Evarts, January 14, 1824, ABCFM-Hawaii Papers, HMCSL; to Rufus Anderson, January 14, 1824, ML, HMCSL.

45. S. Bingham, February 16, 1823, Journal, JC, HMCSL.

46. Levi Chamberlain to Jeremiah Evarts, August 27, 1825, ML, HMCSL.

47. Asa Thurston to the Prudential Committee of the American Board of Commissioners for Foreign Missions, August 16, 1819, ML, HMCSL.

48. William Richards to Jeremiah Evarts, February 2, 1822, ML, HMCSL.

49. Elisha Loomis to Chester Loomis, October 16, 1819, ML, HMCSL.

50. Elisha & Maria Loomis, October 1819, Journal, JC, HMCSL.

51. Artemas Bishop to Jeremiah Evarts, January 30, 1822, ML, HMCSL.

52. Artemas Bishop to Eliza Bishop, November 20, 1821, ML, HMCSL.

53. Daniel & Jerusha Chamberlain to the pastors and brethren of the church of the Sandwich Islands Mission, March 7, 1823, ML, HMCSL.

54. Eliakin Phelps to Jedidiah Morse, March 4, 1819, ML, HMCSL.

55. Daniel Chamberlain, July 1, 1820, Journal, JC, HMCSL.

56. Levi Chamberlain to Joseph Chamberlain, May 8, 1826; to Jeremiah Evarts, October 8, 1821, ML, HMCSL.

57. Hiram Bingham to Calvin Bingham, February 26, 1819; to Samuel Worcester, July 18, 1819, ML, HMCSL.

58. See John A. Andrew, "Betsey Stockton: Stranger in a Strange Land," _Journal of Presbyterian History,_ 52 (Summer 1974) : 157-166. Carol S. Dodd, "Betsey Stockton: A History Student's Perspective," _Educational Perspectives_, 16 (March 1977): 10-15.

59. _Christian Advocate_, February 1823, p. 88.

60. Betsey Stockton noted that while aboard the _Thames_, the Stewarts shared everything with her equally. "The impression such little things [as dividing fruit into thirds] made on my mind will not be easily erased." _Christian Advocate_, May 1824, p. 235.

61. Abraham Blatchely to Jeremiah Evarts, June 17, 1823, ML, HMCSL.

62. Ibid.

63. Betsey Stockton to Levi Chamberlain, December 25, 1824, ML, HMCSL.

64. Ashbel Green, Charles Stewart and Betsey Stockton, October 24, 1822, Document of Duties, ML, HMCSL.

65. Bingham, _Residence_, pp. 60-61.

CHAPTER V

SOJOURNERS AMONG STRANGERS

"If any man come to me, and hate not his
father and mother, and wife, and children, and
brethren, and sisters, yea and his own life
also, he cannot be my disciple. And whosoever
doth not bear his cross, and come after me,
cannot be my disciple."   (Luke 14:26-27)

As the members of the first company prepared to
depart for the Sandwich Islands aboard the Thaddeus in
1819, they could not avoid being subsumed in the greater
cause of foreign mission. They represented the product
of almost three hundred years of Calvinist theology as
they grasped the torch of missionary activity proffered
by a faltering American Board. These young evangelists
were pioneers in the first truly independent American
mission field. It was all heady stuff.

The time for doubts among the missionaries,
themselves, was past. Even as couples shared the
intimacy of marriage vows, the moment belonged less to
them than the greater cause. Indeed, the marriage
requirement made it difficult for respective members to
separate their commitment to a marriage partner from
that to the mission family or the enterprise as a whole.
It was not a time of reflection, but of action. It was
less a time of private dedication than public
acclamation.

The commissioners of the American Board were not
insensitive to the complex emotions of the members of

the Pioneer Company to the Sandwich Islands. Nor were they unaware of the need to reaffirm the necessity for mission to their constituency. The ordination of Thurston and Bingham, their respective marriages, and the departure of the Pioneer Company aboard the Thaddeus offered the opportunity to focus both the missionaries and their supporters on the importance and purpose of the cause.

The Reverend Heman Humphrey delivered the ordination sermon on the text of Joshua 13:1, "that there remaineth yet very much land to be possessed." From the vantage point of the twentieth century this passage seems to be a justification for yet another instance of the transfer of land from its indigenous owners to avaricious Europeans and Americans, but such was not Humphrey's intent. Though Humphrey began his exegesis with a comparison of Israel and the church, saying, "As the land of Canaan belonged to Israel in virtue of a divine grant, so does the world belong to the church," he went on to point out that the church's claim to the world was based on the authority of Christ, and, "the command of Christ is, Go ye into all the world and preach the Gospel to every creature. The most terrible and fatal of all plagues is ravaging all the heathen lands. There is no remedy but the Gospel." In this situation, "the duty of the Church is written in sunbeams. Let her read and obey."[1]

By possession, Humphrey and other missionary adherents meant the spiritual ownership of the land by Christ. That this concept was tied to that of western civilization and the missionaries' own ethnocentric belief in their culture is undeniable, but until very recently such associations were perceived by westerners as a positive benefit of contact. Those believing in the cause of foreign missions wanted to bring unbelievers spiritual blessings and eternal life, but were unable to separate the spiritual from the physical. The approbation they have received from recent generations would have been incomprehensible to most individuals in the early nineteenth century.

Turning his attention to the frontline troops of the missionary enterprise, Humphrey indulged in his own fantasy. "I can fancy that I see [the heathen], hastening down to the shore to welcome you as friends, and as bearers of those 'glad tidings of great joy;' . . . that I behold them gathered around you by hundreds, and listening with silent amazement, while you talk to them of the babe from Bethlehem: -- that I see them casting away their idols and exclaiming with one voice, your God shall be our God, your Savior shall be our Savior." Reluctantly, however, Humphrey conceded that the opposite might occur, "that the [Hawaiians] may meet you with dark and lowering suspicion, and turn away from your instructions with contempt."[2]

Speaking on the occasion of the Bingham marriage two weeks later, the Reverend Thomas H. Gallaudet offered his own thoughts on the purpose of the mission. "This object is to bear the message of a Saviour's love to thousands of immortal souls who have never yet heard of him, and who are plunged in the lowest depths of sensuality and sin; and, also, to introduce the arts and comforts of civilized society." As for those who doubted the wisdom of the enterprise or who whined that there was much to be done at home, Gallaudet reminded them that if the early church had "practiced the same cold-hearted policy . . . of keeping safe at home, and of relieving only the wretchedness which prevails in their own country, doubtless most of us . . . would now be enveloped in the thick gloom of pagan superstition and idolatry."[3]

Whether the rhetoric strengthened the resolve of the first missionaries to the Sandwich Islands or whether it gave them second thoughts as to the wisdom of their actions is unknown. It was too late for faint hearts to turn away. In the words of David L. Perry who gave the final charge to the missionaries, "We have now consecrated you to God and to the heathen. You are, henceforth, dead to the world, dead to the refinements of civilized society, and the endearments of social ties in the bosom of your native land."[4] Or, to paraphrase the words of folk wisdom, the novice missionaries had made their respective cots and now they must lie in them, with or without Clarissa Richards' hoped for "fairy colours."

Yet, later, after the glaring light of publicity had dimmed and after the missionaries had been safely deposited in the Sandwich Islands, they received a letter from Samuel Worcester, secretary of the American Board's Prudential Committee. The letter reveals what more experienced men had known and what each respective missionary privately had castigated in himself or herself. "Missionaries," wrote Worcester, "with all their high privileges and distinctions are still but poor, frail mortals like other men, and like other Christians still in the flesh in continual danger of the evil in their natures warring against the peace of their minds."[5] Indeed, the frailty of missionary resolve had already been noted by Hiram Bingham who delivered a sermon on II Timothy 3:6-7 after the missionary family affirmed the covenant in Boston.[6] The Sandwich Islands offered the missionaries more than a mere personal, spiritual battle. The islands offered physical temptation and mental anguish as these young, inexperienced New England Calvinists dealt with sociological and metaphysical questions that remain unresolved.

II

The New England perception of the missionary task and its implementation were two very different things. The missionaries had first to come to grips with the reality of the native Hawaiians. To these inexperienced New Englanders, no wild man could ever be more feared; no Indian could ever be more different than these, as yet unknown, Pacific people. The New Englanders knew little about the Hawaiians except that they were unbelievers, and to any Christian an unbeliever was, ipso facto, savage, wild, barbarous and degraded. These Calvinists saw the unbeliever as a child of the devil, a creature of darkness, an enemy of God's kingdom.

The situation would have been hopeless except for the examples of Opukahaia and Hopu. The work impossible except for the examples of Eliot and Brainerd. The wild man could be tamed. Writing his brother, Chester, prior to departure, Elisha Loomis stated that the people "at the Sandwich Islands are now in the lowest state of degradation, notwithstanding they are persons of good intellect." Aboard the Thaddeus Captain Blanchard, possibly playing the devil's advocate, told the missionary family that the Hawaiians were degraded, immersed in vice, and "addicted to practices too abominable to be named!" Within sight of his new home, Loomis noted that "our anticipated labors are in a land of darkness as darkness itself. We are to reside among the heathen abandoned to every excess of wickedness. We are to witness the worship of false gods and shall be exposed to a thousand baleful influences."[7]

A closer scrutiny of the Hawaiians did not assuage the New Englanders' apprehension. Upon her first encounter with the natives, Sybil Bingham's heart "failed" her. "Canoes of naked natives are alongside of our vessel . . . . O, my sisters, you cannot tell how the sight of these poor degraded creatures, both literally and spiritually naked, would affect you! I say naked. They have nothing but a narrow strip, which they term a [malo], tied around them." Samuel Whitney was shocked by such limited apparel. "Here is a picture of human depravity, without the covering of a civilized education." Elisha Loomis found the Hawaiians "less disgusting in their appearance than I expected but are almost entirely naked." Nancy Ruggles could only comment that though she had long known of the "heathen," "half of their real wretchedness was never told me." Daniel Chamberlain described the Hawaiians in one word, "Satanic."[8]

The Hawaiians were also noisy. Lucia Ruggles Holman complained, "I have got so tired with the noise and sight of these naked creatures that I could almost wish myself as far from them as you are." Mercy Whitney found that even ashore, "the incessant noise around me is tiring . . . . We hear continual yelling and screaming of natives all day as they swim or run around."[9]

From the perspective of New England sensibilities, little changed in the ensuing three years. When the Thames arrived, Clarissa Richards discovered, she had "often heard of the heathen, -- I had often spoken of them (perhaps with indifference) -- but now I saw them wretched and degraded." Betsey Stockton described the appearance of the Hawaiians as "that of half man and half beast." She remembered that " when they first came on board, the sight chilled our very hearts. The ladies retired to the cabin, and burst into tears; and some of the gentlemen turned pale: my own soul sickened within me, and every nerve trembled." A few months later, after the initial shock had worn off, Miss Stockton would admit "the natives are very pleasant people." Nevertheless, "they are much dirtier than I expected to find them." Levi Chamberlain recalled that "the first sight of the natives on my arrival affected, though it did not surprise me. I was prepared to witness new scenes --to behold ignorance, debasement & wretchedness."[10]

In response to these disturbing scenes the missionaries squared their collective shoulders and committed themselves "to the care and protection of our ever-watchful Heavenly Father, and putting ourselves into the power of strangers and pagans, untutored and destitute almost of their feeling of moral responsibility; intemperate, lewd, and thievish . . . we unhesitatingly entered on this new life among them." Or, as Levi Chamberlain exulted, "I am now on heathen ground. Surrounded by rude barbarians; but though their

Society is not agreeable, I rejoice that I am here . .
. . To benefit them is a service which would dignify an
angel, it will therefore not degrade me."[11]

Initial encounters ashore only served to emphasize
the vast cultural gap between the Hawaiians and the
Americans. When the Bingham party went ashore to meet
with Liholiho at Kailua-Kona on the big island of
Hawai'i, "the multitudiness, shouting, and almost naked
natives, of every age, sex, and rank, swimming, floating
on surfboards, sailing in canoes, sitting, lounging,
standing, running like sheep, dancing, or laboring on
shore, attracted our earnest attention." One wonders
what the Hawaiian reaction was to these serious, white
men in their dark suits. Bingham provides a glimpse of
the Hawaiian response to the American women who
disembarked at Honolulu. The women were the object of
great curiosity on the part of the natives who peered
under the ladies' "projecting bonnets, laughing,
shouting, trotting around with bare feet, heads and
hands."[12]

The first few months were difficult as the
missionaries began their work. At Kailua-Kona, Hawaii
Lucia Holman complained that "the fruits and vegetables
and everything that these islands produce, taste
heathenish." In Honolulu, Sybil Bingham took a more
charitable view. "We find some pleasant traits which
mark the character of this poor people in the midst of
their degradations. Their pacific disposition, their
mild and friendly intercourse with us and with each
other give us hopes of what they will be when the love
of Jesus shall fill their souls." Yet, even the hopeful
Mrs. Bingham experienced disappointment. Two years

after her arrival, Sybil Bingham called on the queen (probably Ka'ahumanu) who was occupied with playing cards and gambling. "As I stood and looked upon the sable group of ignorant, unconcerned, yet precious immortals, thought of their indifference to the message of eternal mercy, and their entire devotions, not only to vain but to sensual delights, my spirit seemed to faint within me."[13]

A month after his arrival in 1823 Charles Stewart took a more positive view. Despite the continued signs of degradation, the first company had made great strides since their arrival. Stewart confidently concluded that "no pagan nation on earth can be better prepared for the labour of a Christian Missionary; and no herald of the cross could desire a more privileged and delightful task, than to take this people by the outstretched and beckoning hand, and lead their bewildered feet into paths of light and life, of purity and peace."[14]

It was difficult for the missionaries to know whether they were making progress or not, but they had firmly established themselves by 1828. The leading ali'i (chiefs) favored the new Christian religion, and the people were inclined to follow their chiefs. Yet there was always the question of whether the enthusiasm for Christianity was the result of a true change of heart. In their report to the American Board in 1828, William Richards and Lorrin Andrews, a member of the Third Company arriving in 1828, were cautiously optimistic in their assessment of the state of the Hawaiians.

> In heathenism, we see all that is noble and elevated in a rational being, commingled with all that is mean, sensual and beastly. The soul that secretly aspires after immorality, can here gratify

its desires, only by momentary and sensual enjoyment. In short, it so resembles chaos in its constituent parts and perfect disorganization, that none but the Almighty power can resolve it to order. This, we believe, he has begun to do.[15]

III

Much to everyone's astonishment, it was not the Hawaiians or the beach community which would offer the greatest temptations to the struggling missionary family. The viper came from within, and his seeds of destruction reaped a harvest of discord and soul-searching at a time when the untried evangelists were least able to deal with it. "If it were the enemy," Hiram Bingham observed, "we could have set ourselves to the battle & in the name of our God defy his assault. But from within, the door is opened, & great does he deem his advantage!" The seemingly purposeful defection of Dr. and Mrs. Thomas Holman, "who after the most unwearying and faithful efforts to reclaim them still manifest[ed] a determination to pursue a course obviously wrong" brought the entire enterprise to the brink of disaster.[16]

When Thomas and Lucia Holman joined the pioneer company, its departure was in danger of indeterminate delay, because the evangelists lacked a physician. Samuel Ruggles thought of his sister, Lucia, and her suitor, a physician practicing in Cooperstown, New York. If the doctor could be persuaded to join the missionary cause, events could proceed on schedule; Lucia could marry, and the Ruggles would have the company of kin on this awesome endeavor.

Lucia Ruggles at twenty-six years of age was an independent and strong-minded woman. She was not indifferent to religion or the cause of foreign missions. Miss Ruggles' brother, Samuel, was a teacher at the Foreign Mission School at Cornwall, Connecticut and she had been active in the [Hawaiian] Society of Butternuts, a fundraising organization for the Cornwall school, prior to opening a girls' school in Cooperstown. There Miss Ruggles met Dr. Thomas Holman, a recent graduate of Cherry Valley Medical School in New York. The couple fell in love, but could not marry due to the debts incurred by the doctor's unsuccessful practice. Then the solution appeared in the guise of becoming missionaries. Reportedly refusing his father's offer of $3000.00 to clear his debts, Dr. Holman signed on with the American Board.[17] The Prudential Committee assumed the debts, purchased the necessary medical books, instruments, drugs and supplies, and sent Holman to Cornwall for training.

Upon initial acquaintance, all seemed to be well between the doctor and his new associates. Hiram Bingham stated that Holman presented "very solid testimonials as a discreet, [sic] solid, & pious young man, devoted to the cause of Missions and qualified to be useful both as a Christian and a physician among the heathen." Holman's training commenced in May 1819. By August, Herman Daggett, the school's master, observed to Samuel Worcester, Secretary of the Prudential Committee, that the doctor had a disposition given to complaints and that he needed to learn humility. Even Samuel Ruggles told Lucia's fiancee that if he could not bring himself to live in harmony with the mission family and the rules under which they lived, he had better stay at home.[18]

Of course, if Holman had taken such advice, he would have lost his bride and regained his debts. The couple married in September and departed aboard the Thaddeus in November 1819. Bingham later placed much of the blame for the disruptions caused by the Holmans on the staff of the Foreign Mission School. Bingham asserted they should have withheld their approval of Holman's candidacy until they knew he could resist temptation and walk the true path. But the staff had had no real choice. If they had rejected Holman, the entire enterprise would have been held back for want of a doctor. Besides, they must have reasoned, the doctors' brother-in-law was Samuel Ruggles, a man of proven integrity and religious zeal. Surely, that would mean something.[19] The American Board had declared at its Sixth Annual Meeting in 1815 that every missionary employed by the American Board was to be solely dependent on the Board for support and that any earnings by a missionary and/or his wife became the property of the Board for the greater object of the missionary cause. Further the American Board stated that at any missionary station with more than one missionary, all salaries, presents and possessions would be part of a common stock. There would be no individual ownership of property or supplies, and no individual wealth. All was subsumed within the greater cause of mission.[20]

The instructions issued by the Prudential Committee to those missionaries departing for the Sandwich Islands in 1819 further bound the participants even as they admonished the small band. The instructions emphasized that "if a Christian is devoted to Christ, the minister is especially devoted & the missionary even more so."

The first point stressed to each individual, "if you have renounced the world, be sure it is without reserve. It is hard enough to live the divine life here. What will you do there if you aren't devoted heart, soul & body to Christ?" The contract between the evangelists and the American Board was based on this renunciation and was valid only so long as the individuals conformed to the instructions which reiterated the 1815 ruling. The Prudential Committee realized that "living so close to one another and so far from the world, there will be disaffections. Brotherly love may only continue via much vigilance, much prayer, crucifixion of self & sanctifying grace." It was expected that the missionaries would do all within their power to strengthen the ties of their fledgling church and mission family even as they fulfilled the tasks of bring literacy, "civilization," and "Eternal Life" to the unbelieving Hawaiians.[21]

The binding was not as strong as the majority of members had hoped. Thomas and Lucia Holman allegedly began almost immediately to disrupt the unity other members of the young mission family found so vitally important. During the voyage the Holmans began to express their intention of acquiring property in Hawai'i and then returning to America. The doctor stated that he had not understood the instructions at the time of embarkation and that he "did not now nor did he ever feel it to be his duty to engage to hold his earnings or his art, at the disposal of the Board or of the mission, in such a sense that he could not if he pleased acquire personal property & return at pleasure to his native land."[22]

Such sentiments shocked Bingham and the others. Holman now clearly stated that it had never been his intention to spend his life in the field, and that while his services to the mission would be free, others must pay. "But," sputtered Reverend Bingham, "the plan of this mission, & the unequivocal instruction of our Patrons do not allow us to set up private wealth as an object." The doctor responded, "You know very well the situation we were in, when those instructions were given. -- I did not understand them; & I question whether you did yourself at the time." Bingham protested that he "did understand them -- they were such as I was looking for, -- such as I had long desired, & such as I was glad to hear." "But I," asserted Thomas Holman, "do not feel myself bound by them any further than they accord with my original plan. I felt willing to spend a few years in the practice of physic among the heathen, -- & if my services would aid the mission, & promote the civilization of the natives, I should be glad of it. But why should you feel concerned about my earnings unless you think I can earn more than the rest." There was little more to be said in the face of such blatant factiousness. The mission family hoped that if they behaved with kindness and forbearance and received the assistance of divine blessing, the young man might be "reclaimed, reformed & saved."[23]

The doctor's bride also gave some cause for concern. The couple's absorption in each other, and the groom's extreme attentiveness to his wife's every desire were offensive to the others. Public displays of affection seemed an affront to the greater purpose of the journey. Despite such secular interests, however,

Lucia Holman was not unaware of the great work, and if she did not completely relinquish her past life, neither did she cling to it.

"This year," confided Mrs. Holman on December 31, 1819, "has witnessed the most trying yet interesting scenes of my life. A new course is marked out for me to pursue : new hopes, new joys, and new sorrows are before me. I often review with pleasure the past scenes of my life, tho this pleasure is mingled with regret that they are never more to be realized." As to her new tasks among the Hawaiians, the young woman exclaimed, "Yes, with the eye of faith I can look forward to the day when the sons & daughters of [Hawai'i] . . . shall become the true & humble followers of the Prince of Peace." Later, Mrs. Holman decided that she was not the one to effect such a change, but aboard the <u>Thaddeus</u> her sentiments and apprehensions were little different from those of her missionary sisters.[24]

Mrs. Holman did deviate, however, in her shipboard activities. Lucia Holman did not attend the sessions led by Mrs. Bingham and Mrs. Thurston to instruct the ladies in grammar, rhetoric, and geography. She, too, had been a teacher and felt no need of the lessons, especially when she suffered from seasickness. But the absence was noted and served to isolate Mrs. Holman from the other ladies.

Mrs. Holman also had poor relations with Reverend Bingham. Bingham accused Mrs. Holman of hoarding fruit which her brother, Isaac Ruggles, had given her in Boston. She defended her position, but the seeds of suspicion were planted. Dr. Holman later accused Bingham of telling his wife that she was "an improper person for a missionary."[25] Whether or not the Holmans had any aptitude for mission, they seemed to have had none at all for diplomacy. By the time the Thaddeus arrived at Kailua-Kona on the Big Island of Hawai'i, the couple had alienated most of the company. Only the Ruggles could still be counted as friends.

When Liholiho agreed to the establishment of a mission station at Honolulu, he stipulated that the doctor would remain with him. Not wishing to leave the Holmans alone in their new situation, the Reverend Asa Thurston and his wife, Lucy, also remained at Kailua-Kona. In retrospect, Bingham and Thurston testified that Holman selected the Thurstons and Thomas Hopu as companions. The doctor recalled that ballots were cast, and that Thurston was not pleased when the assignment came to him. The remainder of the mission family went on to O'ahu, but "it was expected, it was said & the Dr. understood it so . . . that with respect to the family proceeding to [O'ahu] in case of fever, or in other case of urgency, it would be his duty to visit them." The cases of "urgency" were primarily the confinements of several of the wives. It was the expectation of such events which had made the inclusion of a physician so important to the company.[26]

Meanwhile, Dr. Holman attended one of the king's wives and several of his servants, all of whom recovered. Had the doctor failed, his life could have been forfeit. Inasmuch as he succeeded, the Holmans received gifts and provisions which they only occasionally shared with the Thurstons. The doctor also enjoyed some influence with the king, but did not utilize this advantage in extending the gospel. "Never

. . . had a medical man a better opportunity to make a good impression as a pioneer of science, civilization, and Christianity, than he enjoyed," Bingham wrote, but the doctor threw away such opportunities. Relations between the Holmans and the mission family remained strained. Thurston and Bingham corresponded on the doctor's growing alienation and spirit of divisiveness.[27]

The Holmans and the Thurstons often shared only the barest civility. Lucy Thurston wrote Sybil Bingham of an altercation over the issue of sharing water at which Dr. Holman clearly stated his intentions to live in his own dwelling, "that it was not his intention to remain a member of the mission -- that at a future period he intended to return to his native country -- that the medicines in his possession he considered his own." Holman also spoke of "the dignity of his profession -- the superiority it bore contrasted with Mr. T's -- & his being made instrumental of this mission's being received & so comfortably situated." It was all very upsetting to people believing in the unity of Christ.[28]

While Dr. Holman concerned himself with his secular profession, his wife fluctuated between her Christian commitment and human frailties. Even aboard the Thaddeus, "at a time when each of the family needed the support of the others, [Mrs. Holman] allowed herself to express a seeming regret that she had embarked." The others expressed no verbal doubt of their calling and kept their fears to themselves. Reverend Bingham remonstrated with Mrs. Holman on this topic with some good effect, but when the doctor learned of the conversation, he found the reproof to be an "ungentlemanlike abuse of a delicate female."[27]

Lucia Holman's second thoughts became stronger as she encountered her first mission station. The culture shock was intense for the entire mission party, but, once again, Mrs. Holman was the only one to express a desire to leave the mission family. Lucia Holman verbalized her reactions to Lucy Thurston. "I do not find things here as I expected," Lucia confided to her colleague, "I do not feel for the heathen in being among them as I formerly did -- reading or hearing of their miseries -- If there are any that do feel for [the Hawaiians]," she went on, "& possess that self-denying spirit which is necessary to live among them & do them good, I am glad of it -- It is for them to do the work -- But, as for myself I do not possess these feelings & consequently cannot be useful among them -- & I intend to embrace the first opportunity to return to my native land." Mrs. Holman had gone beyond a mere apprehension that she did not possess the proper spirit. She now declared "she would never be willing to exercise that degree of self-denial, which was called for" by the situation. Such thoughts might be honest, and the conclusions logical, but they were not appreciated.[30]

Lucia Holman's ambiguous commitment was further taxed by physical privations the others endured in silence. Kailua-Kona is on the dry side of the Big Island of Hawai'i. Water was five miles away from the mission station. There was no arable garden land and few fresh provisions. The stress of environmental change, physical labor and mental tension took its toll on an already tenuous commitment. Lucia's position became increasingly ambiguous as she began to complain of her health and the desire for plentiful water, good

food and agreeable company. At the end of the summer
Lucia wrote that in all her "trials of sickness and
privations by sea & land, I have never regretted my
undertaking," and, yet, unlike others in the company,
she would be pleased to return home again. "Could any
female" Lucia further reflected, "have known before she
left home, all the trials and afflictions through which
she must inevitably pass, she would not of herself have
strength or grace to enlist in so great an enterprise.
I think," she went on," I may say the same of men." Two
months later Mrs. Holman elaborated on that theme,
saying that "it was pride & selfishness and the desire
of a great name that influenced every one of the mission
family to come out here [to Hawai'i]."[31]

The doctor had an over abundance of pride and a
fractious nature, but his wife possessed verbal
expression that was thoughtless and sharp. It is
difficult to say which was the most distressing to the
mission family. Both represented the enactment of
private doubts and fears that the family sought to deny.
They were a small band in a strange place. They could
not go back; such and act would deny their calling and
perhaps their conversion. It was not a question of
making a mistake, but of eternal salvation. The charge
of seeking fame was easily denied, but the greater issue
of coming out for personal gain, i.e., the assurance of
salvation, raised the question of motive. If the
motivation were even slightly self-interested, then all
sacrifice was for nought and damnation more than
probable. It was, indeed, a psychic disaster to listen
to the Holmans. Such a situation could not continue.[32]

The tension between the Holmans and the mission family reached crisis proportions when the Holmans moved to Lahaina, Maui without the approval of the church. The move touched on four issues of which the major point was the question of authority. The ostensible reason for the move was Lucia Holman's health. The couple went to Lahaina rather than Honolulu, because that was where the king granted them permission to travel. In the uproar of moving, Dr. Holman failed to appear for Maria Loomis' confinement. As a result of flouting authority, placing the missionary enterprise in jeopardy, and endangering the life of Mrs. Loomis, the Holmans were placed under censure.

If there is blame to be fixed, it would seem to revolve around Lucia Holman and the high regard her husband had for her. Unlike the resourceful Lucy Thurston, Lucia felt increasingly overwhelmed by her calling and was quickly disillusioned. She did not have any particular affinity for the Thurstons, and later wrote Samuel Ruggles that isolation among the Hawaiians was preferable to "the society of [those] who feel and conduct towards me as if a stranger." In short, Mrs. Holman was unhappy and unsuited to her new environment. In fact, she had expressed her desire to depart almost upon arrival, causing Reverend Bingham to respond "in his usual taunting way get away if you can!" (Bingham denied this alleged conversation.) Dr. Holman testified the move was necessary to protect his wife's health. Bingham and Thurston said Mrs. Holman never mentioned her health problems to her Christian sisters and even admitted her conduct had nothing to do with her health. In a letter to her brother, Lucia insisted that the removal was her desire, "and at first quite contrary to the will of my husband."[33]

From the church's point of view, if the Holmans insisted on leaving Kailua-Kona, they should have appealed for permission from the church and the king, and moved to the main station at Honolulu. The family believed the doctor had made his plans for Lahaina without even informing the Thurstons. This would leave the Thurstons in isolation and raise Liholiho's suspicions, because the king was jealous of Kalanimoku and Ka'ahumanu who were at Lahaina. By angering the king the Holmans placed the entire missionary enterprise in jeopardy. Later the charge was also made that Dr. Holman was becoming increasingly discontented "as he saw the good name of the leaders rising, & gaining influence."[34]

Dr. Holman denied leaving Kailua-Kona by devious means. "Did I not," he queried, "more than once or twice ask the counsel of brother Thurston on the subject?" But Reverend Thurston replied, "in an unfriendly, unbrotherly manner, Thus, 'I don't know' & would not converse with me at that time any more on the subject." The doctor also stated he had made a written request to Honolulu regarding their move to Lahaina and received no reply. The choice of Lahaina was made by the king. The doctor admitted he had moved without mission family permission, but if he had waited, Holman feared the king might have changed his mind.[35]

The charge that Holman had placed his own interests above those of Mrs. Loomis' health was a harsh one. The doctor declared, however, that he did not attend her confinement, because he was told he was not needed, an assertion both Bingham and Thurston denied. Mrs. Loomis delivered without complications, fortunately.[36]

On July 13, 1820 the brethren issued a united remonstrance signed by Hiram Bingham, Daniel Chamberlain, Samuel Ruggles and Elisha Loomis. They wrote of the fine work Dr. Holman was doing, of his duty to the mission, of his acceptance of the general instructions. After arriving at Lahaina, Dr. Holman responded that he was pleased to be on Maui "and should you see fit to withdraw me from your fellowship & support yet I am confident that God . . . will continue to provide all things necessary for my usefulness, wants & happiness." Lucia Holman's entreaty that her husband should not be censured "for the faults that I have committed" did not soften the tone of Thomas' defiance. The church suspended Dr. Holman from all privileges on August 8, 1820 and placed him under censure pending a fuller investigation. In the interim, the doctor was expected to continue to fulfill his medical obligations.[37]

Lucia Holman continued to waffle. Shortly after the move to Lahaina, Lucia tried to mend her fences with Lucy Thurston. "I verily believe that great good can be affected among [the Hawaiians] with proper means -- but I need not tell you never to expect that from me. I only ask your charity to believe that I do not intend to do any harm." Indeed, this contrite woman was "willing to live forgotten among mankind if I can live in peace -- enjoy the pleasures of a quiet conscience -- void of offense towards God & man." Not surprisingly, her plea fell on deaf ears. Thomas Holman wrote that his wife did not receive the interest or sympathy she had expected causing a decline in both her health and spirits. "Should she continue in this frame of mind, with no more prospect of relief, I shall feel it my absolute duty to return [to the United States] with her."[38]

The evidence seemed to be mounting that the Holmans were looking for a way out of their obligation. Surely the removal to Maui was indicative of this intent. Lucia Holman disagreed. "We never thought nor spoke of separating from the Mission," she wrote prior to her husband's suspension. "No! Far be it from me or my dear husband to wish to separate from this family." But should the brethren decide to separate, "I will feel myself happy to be alone."[39]

Alone, the Holmans would soon be. The family tried to sort out why the Holmans had moved -- whether from maliciousness or misunderstanding. Daniel Chamberlain concluded by November that the Holmans' version was not to be trusted since it changed almost daily. Bingham blamed Mrs. Holman for urging her husband to measures that could only result in censure. Dr. Holman continued to assert that he was doing his duty and was, therefore, neglected and abused.[40]

At length, the family made a decision. Chamberlain questioned Holman closely in order to demonstrate that the doctor's position was without merit. During the questioning Dr. Holman stated: "Mr. Chamberlain. I'd have you know that the blood that runs in my veins was born free, & I'm determined, it never shall be bound by any man." To which Reverend Bingham responded, "We do not wish to change the current of your blood, we only wish you to behave decently." But the time of reconciliation was past. "Your brethren having suspended you from the fellowship without excluding you from the pale of the church, have long waited for you to wipe away the stain & heal the wound, which you have brought upon this little branch of Zion, upon the cause of missions, & on the cause of Christ in general; -- but they have waited in vain -- They have sat down by the turbid waters of Babylon, & waited & wept in vain." Only Mr. Ruggles argued that Dr. Holman be given more time to repent. With sadness and determination, the Reverends Bingham and Thurston drew up the letter of excommunication, charging Thomas Holman with "walketh disorderly" (II Thessolonians 3:6); "slander & railing" (I Corinthians 5:11), and "covetousness" (I Corinthians 5:11). The motion to "publicly, & solemnly, deliver [Thomas Holman] over into the visible kingdom of Satan & declare you and to the world, that you are, & of right ought to be excommunicated from the church of Christ, & no more entitled to the fellowship or the privileges of his kingdom on earth" passed by unanimous vote on January 31, 1821. That same date Lucia Holman was placed under suspension.[41]

Mrs. Holman had received her first admonition on January 16 and made no effort to repent. The church charged Mrs. Holman with persuading her husband to move to Lahaina and declaring that if such were grounds for dismissal, she would rejoice. Such actions were unbecoming in a church member and in a female missionary they constituted "walking disorderly." Lucia was also charged with possessing an improper spirit and manner which manifested itself as "evil speaking." Her greatest crime, however, was the same as the doctor's.

"Any feelings, conduct or expressions, inconsistent with
the full exercise of holy benevolence, are contrary to
the duties which we owe to God & to each other as
subjects of this kingdom. Every particular branch of it
must be governed by the same laws that regulate the
whole." When a member departed from the path of duty,
every effort must be made to reclaim him or her. But
neither Lucia nor Thomas Holman wanted to be reclaimed.[42]

The decision of excommunication and suspension was
a difficult one. Maria Loomis wrote that the "subject
is to painful to dwell on. It is deeply felt by every
member of the family." Bingham lamented "the defection
of Dr. Holman -- Lord what is man!" Samuel Whitney
found Dr. Holman's continued residence with the family
an inconvenience since he did not care to share a meal
with one under excommunication. Whitney was also
Ruggles' associate on Kaua'i, and could scarcely speak
with him on the subject.[43]

The church submitted a report of the charges and
proceedings to the Prudential Committee. Dr. Holman
submitted his version of the dispute, and the family
included their response. In a letter to Bingham, Holman
struck a conciliatory tone, but stated his belief that
"I have not been properly treated, as a brother, a
friend, or a stranger, or even a menial servant of a
commonly good character." In his response to the
charges submitted to the Prudential Committee, Dr.
Holman continued this approach rather than dealing
directly with the charges. An unsigned letter from a
mission family partisan insisted that Dr. Holman's
"paper is altogether offensive in its aspect &
character. He seems to think his own case will appear

fair, if he can attach disgrace to Mr. Bingham." The writer concluded that Thomas Holman did not exhibit "a single expression of genuine grief on account of the unhappy spectacle presented to the heathen -- or of sorrow that he was compelled to leave a mission, to which he had publically [sic] devoted himself, & to which he was bound by the most solemn ties."[44]

The Prudential Committee considered the Holman case at their meeting of June 7, 1821. The committee found that Dr. Holman's reasons for leaving Kailua-Kona were not satisfactory; that he be required to turn over all medicines, medical books, surgical supplies and other American Board property, and that "no person can be considered as belonging to the mission at the Sandwich Islands unless upon the principles expressed in the Public Instructions of the Committee delivered in Boston, Oct. 15, 1819." It remained only to find a suitable ship for the Holman's departure, and to attempt to reclaim Lucia Holman before she, too, was irretrievably lost.[45]

Mrs. Holman, however, remained out of the fold. "We laboured, but in vain, to make her sensible of the dishonor she had brought upon the Church," Elisha Loomis reported. "She maintains that she has conducted herself aright -- that she is unconscious of having slandered the members of the church -- that she has been wronged -- and esteems it her highest happiness that she will one day be able to make known her sufferings to the Christians of America."[46]

In fact, Lucia Holman was enjoying her return to the secular world. Maria Loomis noted that the doctor's wife was receiving presents of every description from the anti-missionary party and left in excellent spirits, seemingly "quite insensitive to the injury she has done & is still doing to the cause of Christ." Reverend Bingham express his distress at Lucia's "pleasure in going home; -- the complacency shown in the multiple attentions of the sea-captains towards her -- the confidence expressed in God -- the joy also at leaving the mission family."[47]

The Holmans departed for Canton aboard the Mentor and ultimately made their way back to Boston via England, arriving in May 1822. The brethren in Hawai'i were "not sorry [the Holmans] have left this place. The extent of the injury they have done this Mission, and the cause of Christ can never be fully known till the great day when all men must give an account to God."[48]

The Holman affair was the most devastating event of the early missionary experience, because it brought the insecurity of Hopkinsian theology to the forefront. The Holmans had been admitted to the band; they had sincerely professed their commitment to God's kingdom. Yet, they not only backslid, they taunted. Their existence made the others question both their motivations and abilities. The Holmans had been erroneously approved by respected members of the church. How, then, could youthful missionaries in a strange culture presume to judge the commitment of a Hawaiian conversion -- or even his or her own. It was imperative to cast the sinners in order to prevent chaos and carry out the mission. Once the Holmans departed, the incident was repressed, but it left a scar which affected the future decisions of the pioneer company.

IV

Despite their internal divisions, the power of the Almighty among the Hawaiians had been displayed for the missionaries from the time of their arrival. Just as God had prepared a place for the Puritans in the wilderness of New England by thinning out the Indian population, He cleared the way for the missionaries in Hawaii two hundred years later. To their intense joy the missionaries aboard the Thaddeus learned that the public religious system of the Hawaiians had been destroyed. "How were our hearts agitated with new and various & unexpected emotions to hear the interesting intelligence, 'Tamehameha is dead' -- 'the Taboos are broken' -- 'The Idols are burnt' -- 'The Moreahs are destroyed' -- and the priesthood is abolished . . . . He who in wisdom has ordained that no flesh shall glory in his presence, has saved us from the danger of glorying in Triumph, & taught us . . . to 'stand still & see the salvation of God.'" Writing his brother, Amos, Bingham observed that these startling events "began to take place soon after the circulation of Obookiah's Memoirs, when a special spirit of united prayer was awakened in the churches of it for these lands." The editors of the Panoplist offered another explanation for the breaking of the kapu system. They suggested that Hawaiians had received news of the British missionary efforts in the Society Islands and were persuaded then that their continued idolatry was both foolish and stupid.⁴⁹

In fact, the breaking of the kapu was the result of Hawaiian domestic politics. The growing commerce between Hawaiians and Europeans and Americans sailing the Pacific Ocean, and particularly the sandalwood trade, had disrupted traditional Hawaiian culture, as

had Kamehameha the Great's wars of unification. With
the men gone for long periods of time, the women were
forced to break kapus on the growing and preparation of
food. The Hawaiians also observed that the foreigners
broke kapus with impunity, and the infractions of the
ali'i often went unpunished. Traditional religion was
under strain when Kamehameha I died in 1819. At his
death the king had named his son, Liholiho, as king
(Kamehameha II) and his favorite wife, Ka'ahamanu, as
kuhina nui, a new office with power equal to the king's.
Ka'ahumanu was pleased with her new position, but
frustrated since many of the major decisions were made
at the sacred heiau (altar) which she, as a woman, could
not enter. Ka'ahumanu, Keopuolani, the new king's
mother, and Hewahewa, the high priest, began to pressure
Liholiho to lift the kapu, effectively destroying the
state support of traditional Hawaiian religion. In this
decision they were supported by the five major chiefs
and their retainers who did not want to lose their lands
during the land redistribution that normally occurred at
the ascent of a new king. In November Liholiho ordered
a feast and pointedly ate with the women symbolizing the
end of the traditional kapu system. The king then
issued orders to destroy the heiaus and burn the idols.[50]

Despite the lack of an official religion the
Hawaiians were in no hurry to embrace a new belief
system. Many still worshipped the old gods, and the
ali'i had not freed themselves of one religion to become
bound to another. The destruction of the state
sanctioned religion, however, had simplified the
missionaries' task, and they praised God for preparing
the way for evangelism.

The missionaries were able to gain attention for their message by their promise to teach literacy and by fortuitous circumstances. Dr. Holman's successful treatment of members of Liholiho's household gained him the gratitude of the king. The Binghams' successful prayers for Ka'ahumanu's recovery in December 1821 brought a respect for the mana, or power, of the New Englanders' religion. The message of Ola Hou, or eternal life, gained a greater audience, but it did not gain converts.[51] Bingham would recall that as their third year among the Hawaiians was ending, the missionaries longed to see the natives "stand up . . . to praise God." However, although their main object was to save souls, the evangelists were distracted by their perceived need to correct Hawaiian manners, improve their modes of dress and living, and remove what the missionaries defined as Hawaiian grossness, wretchedness and destitution. These traits must be replaced by the taste and refinement of western culture. It was a large task contributing "little or nothing in the real work of reform, and leaves the main business of inducing self-denial, repentance, humility, faith and a desire for divine and heavenly things, as difficult and distant as when you began."[52]

In fact, the New England missionaries made little headway until the arrival of William Ellis from the Society Islands. Ellis, of Presbyterian background and under the sponsorship of the London Missionary Society, had been in the South Seas since 1816. Ellis, two colleagues and two chiefly Tahitians arrived in Honolulu on April 16, 1822, enroute to the Marquesas Islands, remaining until August 22. Ellis returned in February

1823 with his wife and two other Tahitian teachers. The assistance of Ellis and his party was immeasurable to the struggling Americans. He had a facility with the Tahitian language that was easily applied to Hawaiian, and communication ceased to be a major barrier. The Tahitian teachers provided the new religion with a legitimacy it had previously lacked. Not only could the Tahitians communicate directly with the Hawaiians, they also had immediate access to the chiefs.[53]

Though grateful for the assistance and distressed by Ellis' departure in 1824, the American missionaries did not place as much stress on the contribution of Ellis and still less on the Tahitians than was probably deserved. Early American efforts to touch Hawaiian hearts had limited results. While at Pu'uloa with Liholiho in 1823 Bingham awoke to find the young king also awake and sought to speak to him of repentance. "I called his attention to the duty of personal and decided piety, and urged the necessity of immediate repentance." But the king replied only that his wickedness was very great and that he would repent in five years.[54]

The educational efforts of the missionaries, called palapala by the Hawaiians, met with considerably greater success. Liholiho had allowed the missionaries to remain for the purpose of teaching the people, and the missionaries were fully aware of the use of literacy as a means of conversion. Bingham encountered a young man who asked him for a book, because of his "desire to learn, my ear, to hear, my eye to see, my hands to handle, for, from the sole of my feet to the crown of my head I love the 'palapala.'" William Richards saw a glimpse of light in the woman who said, "'I have become an old woman and am now very near the grave -- my heart has been hard all the days of my life and I weep when I think of my ignorance: -- I have heard that Jesus Christ can make me better & I have come to you to be taught. Give me a spelling book & learn me the palapala.'"[55]

The situation changed in 1825 when Lord Byron returned the bodies of Liholiho and his favorite wife, Kamamalu, to Hawai'i. The royal couple had gone to London and there succumbed to the measles. In the midst of national anguish and lamentations the missionaries preached on Job 1:21, reminding the people of the fleeting quality of life.[56] The Calvinist perspective as articulated by Bingham was that the sudden death of the rulers was a lesson to the nation. "How impressively did divine wisdom show the vanity of the mirth and wine, the pomp and pride, the distinction and power, of which the departed ones . . . could once boast." God's message was clearly chastising the Hawaiians for putting their trust in princes.[57]

In response, more than one hundred people offered themselves for baptism, including Ka'ahumanu, Kalanimoku, Kalkua, Namahana, La'anui, Kapi'olani, Kapule, Kai'u, Keali'iahonu'i and Richard Kala'aiaulu, all prominent ali'i. Such interest raised the evangelists' hopes of reforming the people as daily inquiries were made on the subject of religion. Samuel Whitney's journal entry of April 5, 1826 tells of a young man who called that evening to tell him "'I am a Sinner, I greatly fear for myself. I begin to pray with trembling anxiety. You know how wicked I have been. I see it now. You used to tell me to forsake my sins and love God, but I did not care for it then, now I feel it.'" Whitney was encouraged by the young man's seeming repentance.[58]

It seemed that at long last the field was ready for the harvest. The missionaries were joyful, but cautious. The Calvinist path to conversion was not an easy one. The problem of how the state of a candidate's heart could be judged and how a genuine conversion could be differentiated from mere enthusiasm became increasingly important.

V

As Hawaiians began to request baptism, a time of joy and hope also became a time of waiting and judgment. Samuel Worcester had clearly set the standards for baptism in his instructions to the pioneer company. "If God, in his infinite grace, prosper your labors, and give you the happiness to see converts to the truth, you will proceed in regard to them, at once with charity and caution. You will allow sufficient time for trial, and for the reality of conversion to be attested by its fruits," so that the "scandal of apostasy may be prevented." The Reverend David L. Perry had warned, "Be not hasty in forming your opinion of the spiritual attainments of the heathen; and do not suddenly receive them into communion with the church. One apostate may do more injury than hundreds who are without."[59]

After excommunicating the Holmans and William Kanui, the missionaries were especially sensitive to the evils of apostasy. About 1821 Thomas Hopu presented one of his students, Holo, as one who had evidence of conversion. Bingham was not convinced. "It is obvious that with so brief and imperfect a knowledge of the provisions and invitations of the gospel, and of the extent and spirituality of the divine law as the people then possessed, it would be no easy matter for them or their teachers to form a well grounded opinion of the presence or absence of a work of saving grace in individual cases of seriousness." Bingham was willing to concede that "human nature is everywhere the same . . . and conversion from sin to holiness . . . must be radically the same in all cases," but he did not baptize Holo. Two years later Bartimus Pua'aki received baptism. Pua'aki had been an attentive hearer of the gospel both at Honolulu and Lahaina for three years. Charles Stewart and William Richards both became convinced of Pua'aki's sincerity and baptized him. It was the second baptism of the mission.[60]

The first baptism was that of Queen Keopuolani as she lay on her deathbed at Lahaina in 1823. The king's mother had invited the Tahitian missionaries into her household at Lahaina, became seriously concerned with the state of her soul and feared damnation. In August 1823 Keopuolani became terminally ill, and the promise of Ola Hou took on greater meaning. Stewart recorded that the king, Ka'ahumanu and Kalanimoku had requested Keopuolani's baptism "saying that it was her earnest and special desire, and that she had only that morning begged 'to be washed with water, in the name of God.' The king urged that she be baptized because "she had the true faith in her heart, had given herself to Jesus Christ long before she was sick" and she had "so earnestly requested it." Ellis, Richards and Stewart concurred on the dying queen's sincerity, and Ellis administered the Christian rite.[61]

Keopuolani was more than the king's mother. She was a sacred chief and represented the highest status of the Hawaiian social, political and religious system. At her death she urged the ali'i to adopt the new religion; entrusted Kauikeaouli (the future Kamehameha III) and his sister, Nahi'ena'ena to William Richards, and urged the king to give up his licentious life and follow the new ways.

The impact of Keopuolani's conversion and baptism could not have been greater. Kalanimoku and Hoapili, her former husbands, converted immediately and there was serious interest among both chiefs and people in the evangelical message. Nevertheless, Levi Chamberlain cautioned the American Board that although Christ's banner had been erected, the people's hearts had not yet been won. "Little can be said confidently of the conversion of a single individual among all this people, though much may be said of the attention of some to the means of grace."[62]

Charles Stewart expressed more confidence in the situation. "Such hopes, and such causes for high expectation, from this people, give sweetness to the Missionary Life." It was a great consolation for the laborers at the ends of the earth to know that if they had not forsaken all they held dear, "these very individuals, now so indescribably interesting, would still have been groping in the thickest shades of spiritual death."[63]

The fact that these people had become interesting, however, did not mean they were worthy to receive baptism. In 1824 when Ka'ahumanu first requested baptism, Bingham hesitated. How terrible it would be if

she later apostatized. Despite her sincerity of
interest, "we dared not authorize such a step till we
had more decisive evidence that she had been born from
above by the power of the Spirit of God." Plainly put,
these Calvinist missionaries, like their Puritan
ancestors, "had no confidence in baptismal regeneration,
or the efficacy of consecrated water to wash away sin.
Nor did we baptize any hearers of the Gospel, merely
because they were hearers, or, as such, asked to be
baptized."[64] In his memoirs Bingham defended himself
from the charge that the early missionaries had been too
slow, and too strict in their admission of candidates
into the church by falling back on traditional Calvinist
theology.

> Believing that conversion brings the subjects of it
> not only to worship God in truth, and to love his
> law, but makes those kind and liberal-hearted who
> were before naturally and habitually covetous, and
> enlists oppressors in the noble business of seeking
> the best good of their dependents, and promotes
> equity in judges and rulers, and true loyalty in
> subjects, I was slow to invite to the Lord's table
> those whose lives furnished no evidence of this
> sort that they had been born from above. At the
> same time I did not suppose any new test of
> character, unknown to the sacred writers, ought to
> be set up.[65]

Bingham was not alone in his concern. In 1826
William Richards wrote the American Board that he "had
been growing particularly anxious lest the people should
settle down satisfied with the more outward performance
of the duties of Christianity, to the neglect of that
which alone can save the soul." Those without true
knowledge of God had no idea of repentance, while those
cognizant of God's character prayed for the cleansing of
their hearts. Richards advised caution in admitting

members to the church in order to avoid the spectre of apostasy, as had occurred in Tahiti. Standards became more severe in Lahaina in 1828 than in New England.

Richards wrote the American Board that under orthodox rules they could have one hundred fifty church members, but they were proud that none of their fifty members had ever been disciplined. The same standards prevailed at Kailua-Kona where Asa Thurston asserted that none should be baptized until he or she was well instructed in grace and the fruits of their repentance well established. These rules must prevail even when the missionaries believed the Holy Spirit had touched an individual. Joseph Goodrich, stationed at Hilo, agreed, observing that "many have come desiring to be baptized, and admitted into the church, and to follow on to know the Lord. Their lives, and conversation, have been blameless, for more than a year past; yet," he continued, "I feel, that the utmost caution is necessary, lest I should judge amiss, and be too hasty, in admitting them into church communion with us."[66]

Such caution was well in keeping with the Calvinist theological and evangelical missionary tradition, but it did not give the **Missionary Herald** much news to share with the friends of mission. Bingham reported that on April 24, 1828 there were eighty-two members of the Hawaiian church, thirty-two Americans and fifty Hawaiians. Such low numbers did not justify the size and expense of the mission. Nor did they coincide with the New Haven theology or "new measures" that were changing the American approach to conversion. The third, fourth and fifth companies of missionaries arriving between 1828 and 1832, came of age in a different America from the earlier missionaries, and they had a different approach to the qualifications of conversion. By 1832 the church had admitted six hundred Hawaiians.[67]

VI

Life was difficult on missionary ground. It was filled with frustrations, mental and spiritual, as the missionaries struggled to come to terms with themselves, their God and their flock. Those who remained in the field had no second thoughts as to their vocation, though some doubted their ability to do the job. On his thirty-fifth birthday, October 30, 1824 Hiram Bingham wrote his parents that "the great Lord of the harvest is still exceedingly good to me & mine. I am still happy in my family & happy in my work & encouraged with the hope that our labor will not be altogether in vain." Samuel Whitney discovered that the work of a missionary was hard, "but it is a work I love & in which I hope to live and die." Yet on New Year's Day 1822 Whitney wrote, "Where hath been my stupid heart? What have I done for the poor heathen? . . . What bearing will my connection with them have in the Eternal world?"[68]

Daniel Chamberlain, a man who seldom confided his thoughts to paper, wrote the mission church shortly before his departure, "I entered upon the work . . . with joy & trembling -- with joy that my highest wishes were gratified . . . with trembling lest I should do dishonour to the holy cause in which I had professedly engaged." Chamberlain was conscious that in may ways he had failed and asked the congregation's forgiveness, "feeling that it becomes me to lie low in the dust before God and humbly to ask for his pardoning mercy."[69]

Levi Chamberlain was a man of great piety and dedication who, to his frustration, served as the secular agent for the mission because of his business experience. Writing his friend Rufus Anderson in 1825 Chamberlain reported that the mission prospered, but lamented, "I wish I could tell you that I am doing as much as I ought to help it forward." There might be those who thought missionaries were close to angels. "Alas! I feel that I am hardly a Christian; -- and so far from possessing the spirit and tempo of those holy spirits, . . . I do not even deserve to be honored as a helper to the least engaged in missionary spirit." A year later Levi Chamberlain wrote his brother, Joseph, "Never was I more [happy], -- I would not exchange the labor, toils, privations, & sufferings of missionary life for all the wealth & honors of the world." Though Chamberlain would often reflect on his unworthiness as a Christian and a missionary, he had no desire to do anything else.[70]

Nor did Chamberlain's friend and colleague, Charles Stewart. Writing to his friend, Levi, after six months in Hawai'i, Stewart observed, "We have from our own experience learned that it is a vastly different thing to be a Missionary at home in America & be a Missionary abroad at the Sandwich Islands. How have we sustained the shock of that difference? -- In my opinion we may congratulate ourselves as being happy indeed if it had only made us more devoted." A month later Stewart lamented that he and Chamberlain seldom saw each other. "Missionary ground I find to be far more dangerous ground than I anticipated, and, at times, I can scarce help weeping at the evils which not only creep into our hearts but which threaten to influence my actions & cover us with shame. I never knew the weakness of Christian character till I embarked in my present enterprise." Yet, Stewart hoped that what he had felt and seen had purified his missionary spirit. "I feel more willing . . . to be anything, to do anything & to suffer anything that will promote the best interests of the Mission as a body." Several years after his departure due to Harriet Stewart's health, Charles Stewart reflected that "the happiest days I have ever known or ever expect to know on earth, were those of my residence as a missionary at the Sandwich Islands."[71]

Several of the women were of much the same mind, despite their greater hardships. Martha Goodrich confided to Nancy Ruggles that she still entertained some doubt as to her capabilities. "O, that I could feel as I ought the importance of being truly devoted to the work and service of God among these poor ignorant fellow immortals."[72]

The women had an additional cause for frustration and discomfiture. Expecting to share in the missionary enterprise, many were distressed to be so taken up with domestic concerns that they had little time to spread to the gospel. One of Sybil Bingham's first students was the Hawaiian wife of an American. "Some little seasons spent with her in unfolding the first principles of christianity, have been exceedingly interesting. It has awakened missionary zeal when exhausting labours have smothered it." Mercy Whitney would exclaim after explaining John 14 and 15 to one of the king's companions, "I have never felt more engaged in the Missionary work then in the short time I have spent

instructing this heathen youth." Louisa Ely asked
Elizabeth Bishop, "What can be pleasanter than to labor
to enlighten the dark minds of these ignorant heathen?
For this people [Opukahaia] in his dying moments, wept
and prayed."[73]

Pleasant as these interludes were, however, they
were few. In 1824 Sybil Bingham confided her
disappointment to Lucy Thurston that there was "so much
apparent necessity for having so much to do with the
vain world." Six years later Mrs. Bingham wrote Fanny
Gulick, "I have had occasion, many times in ten years,
to quiet myself with the thought, that manual labor,
when given to do in the providence of God . . . would be
accepted in the good work." After eight years in the
field, Mercy Whitney wrote Lucy Thurston that she
"sometimes almost despaired of ever doing very much more
for the heathen, except by example." Two years later,
Mrs. Whitney wrote her sister, Maria Partridge,

> I do think if I may judge from my own experience &
> observation, that greater degrees of grace are
> necessary to keep the soul in a spiritual frame &
> enable a person faithfully to discharge his duty,
> far separated from christian society, surrounded by
> everything appalling to the eye & sickening to the
> heart, than when enjoying frequent intercourse with
> christian friends. My views in this respect are
> altered materially, from what they were before I
> left A[merica] when imagination fancied, that the
> Missionary whose object was only to evangelize the
> heathen, & promote their spiritual welfare, could
> he enjoy that which it was his daily labor to
> propagate. But I have once & again had occasion to
> mourn over a cold stupid, heart, almost
> inactive & lifeless, in the things of religion. I
> do think that when a missionary is enabled to live
> as he ought, he experiences a joy & satisfaction
> which the mass of professing christians in
> civilized lands seldom attain.[74]

Mercy Whitney, however, thought a missionary was seldom able to live as he ought.

VII

Despite such personal disillusionment, the missionaries remained committed to the cause of spreading the gospel. In 1827 Asa Thurston and Artemas Bishop wrote a joint letter to Jeremiah Evarts stating that the discouragements of the missionary field "ought not to lessen the exertions of the friends of Jesus to furnish the heathen with the bread and water of life. How many and how great soever the obstacles which meet us in evangelizing the nations, they can never remit the obligations of Christians to furnish the world with the means of salvation."[75]

The mission field was not totally without its compensations. Writing Rufus Anderson from the station at Kawaihae in 1826, Artemas Bishop had declared, "could you but witness for one day the order, the attention, the anxious eager look and observe the starting tear that starts in the eye of the tawny sunburnt savage, and the look of hope and joy as he casts his look upwards to heaven upon hearing the terms of pardoning mercy . . . your heart would leap for joy."[76]

Life in the field, however, did affect the opinions of the missionaries regarding the basic qualifications future candidates for the office should meet. As early as 1821 Samuel Whitney observed to a young relative that in this vocation "ardent personal piety is a requisite, without this . . . he is of all men most miserable." A missionary also needed a spirit which could look danger and death in the face. He required diligence and perseverance amidst discouragement and depravity, weakness and humility amidst success and honor. "In short, one who can become all things to all men, . . . continually look to God as the Author and finisher of his faith, with a heart full of love to God and the souls of the Heathen." The Reverend Artemas Bishop seems to have been thinking of interpersonal relationships within the mission family when he made the recommendation to the American Board in 1824 that future missionaries "must be prepared for self-denial, especially the greatest of all self-denial, a willingness to submit their opinions in every instance . . . to the voice of the mission."[77]

Writing the American Board a year later, Levi Chamberlain disclosed his advice for the entire missionary enterprise. Regarding the mission family in Hawaii there three major needs; first, a need for "a supremely devoted spirit -- a spirit of self-denial & missionary enterprise;" Secondly, a need for "more love to the heathen, & more of that spirit of prayer;" third, came the need for the "prayers of patrons, helpers & the Christian church -- and lastly, we need the means, -- the pecuniary means." Chamberlain then turned to the need for more missionaries, "laborers of the true stamp -- persons that are qualified to preach, and who are willing to suffer the loss of all things for Christ -- who are willing to become all things to all men, and . . . who are willing to be nothing."[78]

Joseph Goodrich echoed his brother missionary's concern. "A population of nearly 40,000 souls have open ears to hear the Gospel. And must they be left to perish . . . crying for someone to come, and show them the way to eternal joy and peace? Must they be left to perish, because American Christians have exhausted their charities?" Clearly more laborers were needed.[79]

"We hope," wrote James Ely, "there are many who are of the true stamp -- who are devoted to the cause and who will follow [Christ] through evil and through good report." However, Ely did not want the American Board to be swayed by the enthusiastic zeal of those who were influenced by the romantic picture of the missionary surrounded by adoring natives. "A true missionary who is moved by love to [Christ] and his kingdom -- who looks on the work of propagating the gospel as self-denying work -- who calculates for perils, and hardships, privations, and disappointments -- and who girds on his armor and resolves to stand by [Christ] and his cause in dangers and deaths," was what the field needed.[80]

None of the missionaries who remained in the field regretted his or her acceptance of the call. Many of those who were forced by ill-health to leave the field did so with despair. It was difficult, according to Levi Chamberlain, to decide whether a missionary "shall remain on missionary ground with certain death before [him or her] and a termination of all [his or her] usefulness" or return to the United States where he or she could restore his or her health and labor elsewhere in the Lord's vineyard."[81] After the death of Elizabeth Bishop in 1828, the mission family generally preferred to send its ailing members back to Boston than face the spectre of another untimely death.

Regardless of their length of time in the field, however, all experienced shock at the great disparity between their expectations of the missionary life and the actual conditions they encountered. It was one thing to read of David Brainerd's hardships, and quite another to experience them. For many years the example of Opukahaia bore little resemblance to the behavior of his countrymen.

The missionaries put aside their illusions and grew into adulthood, but accepted the decisions of youth. For those who remained in the field, and many of those who departed, the cause of spreading the gospel remained a sacred duty. But their discoveries about the harsh realities of evangelist's life and about each other led them to offer the preceding advice as to the recruitment of future workers. These people needed to be filled with faith and zeal, but rather than perceiving the role of missionary as that of the brave martyr, the candidates must be made to realize that the missionary path was one of humility and self-denial, of thorns rather than roses. Mercy Whitney summed up this experiential understanding in a letter she wrote after eight years as a missionary on Kaua'i.

> How many enlist in the cause with a very inadequate knowledge of themselves, or of the work before them. Far be it from me to discourage anyone who has a call to engage in a Mission, but I have sometimes thought, had I known as much of my unfitness for such a station before I left [America] as I have since known, I fear I should hardly have dared to enter upon it. I say this not because I am sorry I ever gave myself to the work, or have any desire to return to my native country . . . . But O the obligations & responsibility which rest upon me! Had I not an Almighty arm to lean upon, I fear I should sink at once.[82]

VIII

The question of missionary impact on the indigenous Hawaiians has been amply documented by those who support missionaries as a "civilizing" factor, those who decry their despoliation of indigenous culture and those who purport to take the neutral position.[83] Regardless of the discussion of the relative merits or demerits of missionary influence, however, no one doubts that the New England missionaries caused significant changes in the Hawaiian culture.

The aspects of the western civilization brought by the New England missionaries were very different from those brought by merchants, whalers and seamen from the United States and Europe. The latter had, in general, come to Hawaii in an effort to escape the very cultural mores the former were so determined to introduce. Conflict was constant and inevitable with Hiram Bingham, by virtue of his position as the head of the missionary family and his location at Honolulu, involved in almost every controversy. As news of these altercations drifted back to the United States, the American Board asked how such hostility could be directed towards the mission if its members were following their instructions to refrain from political activity. "Why should one not expect opposition from those who love darkness rather than light," Bingham defended, "whether they are externally white as the polished European or sable as the degraded Ethiopian, or swarthy as the barbarous Polynesian."[84]

As for meddling in politics, the missionaries emphatically denied all such charges. In an explanation clearly revealing its Calvinist roots, Bingham reiterated the Puritan position on the separation of

church and state governing the political participation
of missionaries in the Sandwich Islands. "The ministry
of religion and the ministry of the state each has its
duties; but each in its own order and place, and both
for the glory of the same Master." The state derived
its powers from God, with both rulers and subjects bound
to God's will and the "chief magistrate being
emphatically God's minister." Therefore, the state is
a religious institution. Nevertheless, the state is
not a church. While the state is organized for
self-preservation, the church uses moral means to teach
and illustrate the world of God. In keeping with this
explanation, "the Hawaiian state has had no right and
has claimed no power to appoint the officers, or direct
the action, or control the discipline of the church :
and the church there has had no power and claimed no
right to appoint the officers or control the action of
the state." However, "the ministers both of the church
and state should, if they would be loyal to the Divine
Sovereign, concur in publishing statutes, and in
inculcating the principles of truth, equity, temperance,
and righteousness."[85]

The mission made little headway in evangelism until
Lord Byron returned the bodies of Kamehameha II
(Liholiho) and Kamamalu in 1825. The New Englanders
began to preach with renewed vigor on such topics as the
wages of sin, the need for repentance and the fleeting
quality of life. Yet, these factors were less important
for the growth of religious interest than the regency of
Ka'ahumanu on behalf of the new king, Kamehameha III
(Kauikeaouli). Ka'ahumanu had been interested in the
new religion for sometime, but her possession of two

husbands disqualified her candidacy until she sent away the younger consort, A. Keali'iahonai.

Kaumuali'i, Ka'ahumanu's remaining husband, died in 1824 and left his holdings, not to his son, George Kaumuali'i whom the pioneer company had returned to Hawai'i, but to Kamehameha II (Liholiho). George Kaumuali'i led a rebellion to secure Kaua'i for himself. When the O'ahu chiefs inquired as to the appropriateness of crushing the rebellion, the missionaries declared the conflict to be a just war. With God on their side, the centralizing forces defeated the rebels. Shortly thereafter, in March 1825, Lord Byron arrived.[86]

In June several chiefs, Ka'ahumanu and Kalanimoku among them, presented themselves for baptism. Bingham placed the group on probation. That same month the chiefs decided to patronize the palapala and to suppress vice. In August the chiefs formally prohibited gambling and adultery (including prostitution) and required their people to attend school and church, and to observe the Sabbath.

These restrictions caused immediate hostility among the merchants and whalers who attacked the missionaries both physically and on paper for this blatant meddling in chiefly policy. From the missionary perspective, however, the chiefs were merely exhibiting the fruits of their probable conversions.

The fruit was sufficient for the baptism of the chiefly candidates in the early part of December 1825. On December 12, the new church members bore more fruit as they discussed the feasibility of adopting the Ten Commandments as the national law code. There is no evidence that the missionaries suggested such a formal act, but the connection between missionary teaching and public policy is clear from both New England and Hawaiian perspectives.

Calvinist theology of the Christian commonwealth stressed that Christian officials would naturally apply their faith to public policy. The chiefly interest in applying biblical sanctions to Hawaiian mores was therefore interpreted by the missionaries as the fruit of genuine conversions. But it was more than that.

By 1825 the missionaries had unknowingly proven to the Hawaiians the power of their god, Jehovah. Liholiho had flaunted Jehovah, and he was dead. George Kaumuali'i had not had Jehovah's support in the recent rebellion, and he had lost. Keopuolani, a sacred chief, had urged the acceptance of Jehovah. Clearly the power once held by the Hawaiian gods was now held by Jehovah, and the way to gain Jehovah's blessings was to follow his decrees as interpreted by his representatives, the missionaries.

In 1827 the chiefs issued three laws prohibiting murder, theft and adultery. This marks the beginning of formal legislation in the Hawaiian Kingdom. The law code continued to develop. In a proclamation dated October 7, 1829, Kamehameha III declared, "The laws of my country prohibit murder, theft, adultery, prostitution, retailing ardent spirits at houses for selling spirits, amusements on the Sabbath day, gambling and betting on the Sabbath day, and at all times."[87]

The growing association of government policy with religious instruction demonstrates the extensive cultural changes which took place in Hawai'i between 1825 and 1830. It is unlikely such major changes could or would have occurred without the close association of the missionaries and the ruling chiefs. The missionaries taught the chiefs the same faith they taught the commoners. Yet, they were aware that a chief was inseparable from his office, even as a magistrate was, and that a Christian chief, as a Christian magistrate, could not avoid bearing the fruits of his or her conversion in his or her capacity as a ruling chief. This is precisely the point where church and state, though separate, intersected.

No one would deny that the Calvinist missionaries irrevocably changed Hawaiian culture. The missionaries believed it was a change for the better. Twenty years after his arrival in Hawaii, Hiram Bingham could see the results of missionary toil. "A nation has been raised from blank heathenism to a rank among enlightened nations, to the enjoyment of letters and laws, of Christianity and the hope of heavenly glory." This accomplishment was one to encourage the continuation of the missionary cause throughout the world. "If the American Board and its friends and laborers have not done too much for the nation in a generation past . . . those who are on the Lord's side, grateful for what God has wrought there, will be encouraged to attempt and expect the same . . . for other nations, till, in every tongue, they shall harmoniously hymn the Messiah's praise."[88]

SOJOURNERS AMONG STRANGERS - ENDNOTES

1. Humphrey, op. cit.,pp. 5-7, 18-19.

2. Ibid., pp. 25-26.

3. Thomas H. Gallaudet, An Address . . . (Hartford: Lincoln & Stone, Printers, 1819), pp. 9-10.

4. David L. Perry, The Charge in Humphrey, p. 37.

5. Samuel Worcester to Rev. Mssrs. Bingham and Thurston and Other Members of the Sandwich Islands Mission, June 8, 1820 in the Fifty-seventh Annual Report of the Hawaiian Mission Children's Society (Honolulu, 1909), pp. 55-58.

6. "For of this sort are they which creep into houses, and lead captive silly women laden with sins, led away with divers lusts, ever learning, and never able to come to the knowledge of the truth." (II Timothy 3:6-7 KJV).

7. Elisha Loomis to Chester Loomis, October 16, 1819, ML; March 28, 1820, Journal, JC. M. Whitney, February 20, 1820, Journal, JC, HMSCL.

8. S. Bingham, March 31, 1820, Journal, JC, HMCSL; Samuel Whitney to Eli Smith, March 31, 1820, ML. Loomis, April 1, 1820, Journal. Samuel & Nancy Wells Ruggles, April 1, 1820, Journal. Daniel Chamberlain, April 15, 1820, Journal, JC, HMCSL.

9. Lucia Ruggles Holman, April 3, 1820, Journal, M. Whitney, April 30, 1820, Journal, JC, HMCSL.

10. Clarissa Lyman Richards, April 25, 1823, Journal, JC, HMCSL. Christian Advocate, January 1825, p. 39; May 1824, p. 232. Levi Chamberlain to George Rogers, November 10, 1823, ML, HMCSL.

11. Bingham, Residence, p. 95. Levi Chamberlain to Joseph Chamberlain, April 16, 1823, ML, HMCSL.

12. Bingham, Residence, pp. 86, 95.

13. L. Holman, July 1, 1820, Journal, JC. S. Bingham, July 3, 1820, March 14, 1822 Journal, JC, HMCSL.

14. C. Stewart, Journal, p. 140.

15. Lorrin Andrews and William Richards to Jeremiah Evarts, September 30, 1828, ML, HMCSL.

16. A note on sources. The material on the Holman case is based primarily on two reports sent from the church at Honolulu, Hawai'i to the American Board at Boston. Hiram Bingham and Asa Thurston to S. Worcester, February 15, 1821, TS, HMCSL. Hiram Bingham and Asa Thurston, History of the defection of Dr. Tho. Holman, May 11, 1822, ABCFM-Houghton Papers (hereinafter referred to as ABCFM), HMCSL. Aside from statements by the Holmans, there is no evidence refuting the charges. Hiram Bingham, Journal of Mr. Bingham's Tour to Atooi [Kaua'i], October 1, 1821, ABCFM-Hawaii (hereinafter referred to as ABCFM-H), HMCSL. Elisha & Maria Loomis, Journal, November 28, 1820, JC, HMCSL.

17. H. Bingham & A. Thurston, 1822, p. 16, op.cit.

18. H. Bingham to S. Worcester, May 11, 1819, ML, HMCSL. H. Bingham to J. Evarts, November 2, 1820, ML, HMCSL. Andrew, p. 113, op. cit. Albertine Loomis, Grapes of Canaan (New York: Dodd, Mead & Company, 1951), p. 72. Miller, p. 35, op. cit

19. H. Bingham to J. Evarts, November 2, 1820, ML, HMCSL.

20. Panoplist, November 1815, p. 341

21. Humphrey, pp. ii-iv, viii-ix, op.cit.

22. H. Bingham & A. Thurston, 1822, pp. 26, op.cit.

23. Ibid., pp. 27-29.

24. L. Holman. Journal, (Honolulu, HI: Bishop Museum Special Publications #17, 1931), p. 10.

25. T. Holman to Prudential Committee, May 14, 1822, ABCFM-H, HMCSL.

172

26. H. Bingham & A. Thurston, 1822, pp. 29-30, op. cit. T. Holman to Prudential Committee, November 21, 1820, ML, HMCSL.

27. T. Holman to Prudential Committee, November 21, 1820, ML, HMCSL. H. Bingham, Residence, p. 104, op.cit.

28. H. Bingham & A. Thurston, 1822, pp. 40-41, op.cit.

29. Ibid., pp. 7-8. Bingham went on to say that such a response "has been the fate of every brother or sister who has had the kindness to remind [the Holmans] of their faults." L. Thurston, Journal (Printer's Copy), p. 48, op. cit. H. Bingham & A. Thurston, 1821, p.41, op.cit.

30. H. Bingham & A. Thurston, 1821, p. 41, op.cit.

31. L. Holman, Journal, pp. 37-38, op.cit. D. Chamberlain to S. Worcester, November 14, 1820, ML, HMCSL.

32. See; Henry N. Wieman & Regina Wescott-Wieman, Normative Psychology of Religion (New York: Thomas Y. Crowell Company, 1935). It is suggested that the conversion process brought the regenerate Christian into a cultus which provided him or her with a sense of permanence and continuity. Such proclivities would be especially strong among those who 1) have accepted a missionary calling, and 2) represent a cultural enclave surrounded by non-members. Unity among the members is of primary importance in order to maintain religious and cultural identity. Thus, the Holmans' behavior threatened to upset the delicate balance upon which the members of the mission family based their existence.

33. H. Bingham & A. Thurston, 1821, pp. 111-112, op.cit. L. Holman to S. Ruggles, August 1, 1820, ML, HMCSL.

34. H. Bingham & A. Thurston, 1822, pp. 46-48, op.cit. H. Bingham & A. Thurston, 1821, p. 76, op.cit.

35. Ibid., 1821, pp. 68-69. T. Holman to Prudential Committee, May 14, 1822, op.cit.

36. H. Bingham to S. Worcester, October 11, 1820, ML, HMCSL. H. Bingham & A. Thurston, 1821, p. 70,

op.cit. H. Bingham & A. Thurston, 1822, p. 67,
op.cit.

37. H. Bingham & A. Thurston, 1821, pp. 61-62, 73, 84,
op.cit. L. Holman to S. Ruggles, August 1, 1820,
op.cit. Lucia Holman further insisted, "You may be
assured that my dear husband was not unfaithful to
me on this subject when I entreated him to come [to
Lahaina]." H. Bingham to S. Worcester, October 11,
1820, op. cit.

38. H. Bingham & A. Thurston, 1822, p. 54, op.cit. T.
Holman to Prudential Committee, November 21, 1820,
op.cit.

39. L. Holman to S. Ruggles, August 1, 1820, op.cit.

40. H. Bingham to J. Evarts, November 2, 1820, op.cit.
D. Chamberlain to S. Ruggles, August 1, 1820,
op.cit. T. Holman to S. Worcester, November 21,
1820, ML, HMCSL.

41. H. Bingham & A. Thurston, 1821, pp. 102, 125-132,
op.cit. H. Bingham & A. Thurston , 1822, pp. 68,
100, 111, op.cit. H. Bingham to J. Evarts, January
31, 1821, ML, HMCSL.

42. H. Bingham & A. THurston, 1821, pp. 113-114, op.cit.

43. Elisha & Maria Loomis, Journal, January 16, 1821,
op.cit. S. Whitney, Journal, January 13, 1820, JC,
HMCSL. H. Bingham to Rev. William Jackson, February
1821, ML, HMCSL.

44. H. Bingham & A. Thurston, 1822, p. 22, op.cit.
Unsigned to the Prudential Committee, n.d., ML,
HMCSL.

45. J. Evarts for the Prudential Committee, Minutes re
Holman, June 7, 1821, ML. HMCSL.

46. Elisha & Maria Loomis, Journal, August 14, 1821,
op.cit.

47. Ibid., October 2, 1821. H. Bingham, Journal of Mr.
Bingham's Tour, October 1, 1821, op.cit.

48. Elisha & Maria Loomis, Journal, October 2, 1821,
op.cit.

49. H. Bingham, D. Chamberlain, S. Whitney, S. Ruggles and E. Loomis to S. Worcester, July 23, 1820, ML, H. Bingham to Amos Bingham, January 2, 1820, ML, HMCSL. Panoplist, December 1820, p. 572.

50. Kuykendall, op. cit., pp. 61-70. For a full discussion of the significance of the kapu system and the underlying reasons for its destruction see, Marshall Sahlins, Historical Metaphors and Mythical Realities, (Ann Arbor: The University of Michigan Press, 1981) and Lilikala (Dorton) Kame'eleihiwa, "Land and the Promise of Capitalism: A Dilemma for the Hawaiian Chiefs of the 1848 Mahele," (Ph.D. dissertation, University of Hawaii at Manoa, 1986).

51. (Dorton) Kame'eleihiwa, p. 186.

52. Bingham, Residence, p. 169.

53. See, Dorothy Barrere and Marshall Sahlins, "Tahitians in the Early History of Hawaiian Christianity: The Journal of Toketa," Hawaiian Journal of History 13 (1979), 19-35. Kuykendall emphasizes the importance of native helpers as well as Ellis' contribution. op. cit. p. 103.

54. Bingham, Residence, pp. 178-179.

55. Hiram Bingham to Jeremiah Evarts, January 1, 1824. William Richards to Jeremiah Evarts, June 1, 1824, ML, HMCSL.

56. "The Lord gave, and the Lord hath taken away; blessed be the name of the Lord." (Job 1:21 KJV); Hiram Bingham, Charles Stewart and Elisha Loomis to Jeremiah Evarts, March 14, 1825, ML, HMCSL.

57. Bingham, Residence, p. 267.

58. Ibid. Samuel Whitney, April 5, 1826, Journal, ML, HMCSL.

59. Samuel Worcester, "Instructions given by the Prudential Committee . . . February 7, 1812," in First Ten Annual Meetings of the American Board of Commissioners for Foreign Missions (Boston: Crocker and Brewster, 1834) p. 41. Perry, pp. 34-35.

60. Bingham, Residence, pp. 147-148.

Bingham examined Pua'aki as to his understanding of the Christian religion and recorded both the questions and the answers in his memoirs. These questions and answers represent quite a sophisticated understanding of both Calvinist theology and European/American philosophical concepts for one who had only been exposed to them for five years. "Why do you ask to be admitted to the church? Because I love Jesus Christ, and I love you, and desire to dwell in the fold of Christ, and join with you in eating the holy bread and drinking the holy wine. What is the holy bread? It is the body of Christ, which he gave to save sinners. Do we then eat the body of Christ? No, but we eat the bread which represents his body; and as we eat bread that our bodies may not die, so our souls love Jesus Christ, and receive him for their Savior that they may not die. What is the holy wine? It is the blood of Christ, which he poured out on Calvary, in the land of Judea, to save us sinners. Do we then drink the blood of Christ? No, but the wine represents his blood just as the holy bread represents his body, and all those who go to Christ and trust in him will have their sins washed away in his blood, and their souls saved for ever in heaven. Why do you think it more suitable that you should join the church than others? Perhaps it is not. If it is not proper, you must tell me; but I do greatly desire to dwell with you in the fold of Christ. Who do you think are proper persons to be received to the church? Those who have repented of their sins, and have obtained new hearts. What is a new heart? One that loves God and loves the Word of God, and does not love sin or sinful ways." Bingham, Residence, p. 253. (Bingham's quotation marks have been deleted.)

61. Stewart, Journal, p. 215. (Dorton) Kame'eleihiwa, pp. 187-189.

62. L. Chamberlain to J. Evarts, June 10, 1823, ML, HMCSL. (Dorton) Kame'eleihiwa, ibid.

63. Stewart, Journal, p. 263.

64. Bingham, Residence, p. 214.

65. Ibid., p. 268.

66. William Richards to Jeremiah Evarts, May 5, 1825, ABCFM-Hawaii Papers. William Richards to Rufus Anderson, May 20, 1828, ML, HMCSL. Asa Thurston to unknown, December 10, 1828, ABCFM-Hawaii Papers, HMCSL. Joseph Goodrich, September 23, 1828, Journal, Lyman Museum.

67. Figures in Bradley, The American Frontier, op. cit., p. 145; Hiram Bingham to Jeremiah Evarts, June 12, 1828, ML, HMCSL.

68. Hiram Bingham to Calvin Bingham, October 30, 1824, Bingham Family Papers, HMCSL. Samuel Whitney, March 4, 1821, Journal, JC. January 1, 1822, Journal, ML, HMCSL.

69. Daniel & Jerusha Chamberlain to the pastors & brethren of the church of the Sandwich Islands Mission, March 7, 1823, ML, HMCSL.

70. Levi Chamberlain to Rufus Anderson, August 17, 1825, to Joseph Chamberlain, May 8, 1826, ML, HMCSL.

71. Charles Stewart to Levi Chamberlain, November 22, 1823, December 28, 1823, to Jeremiah Evarts, June 8, 1829, ML, HMCSL.

72. Martha Goodrich to Nancy Ruggles, March 29, 1826, Lyman Museum

73. S. Bingham, July 22, 1820, Journal. M. Whitney, July, 22, 1821, Journal, JC. Louisa Ely to Elizabeth Bishop, May 14, 1824, ML, HMCSL.

74. Sybil Bingham to Lucy Thurston, January 1824, Bingham Family Papers; to Fanny Gulick, September 4, 1830, ML, HMCSL. Mercy Whitney to Lucy Thurston, January 27, 1828; to Maria Partridge, March 24, 1830, ML, HMCSL.

75. Asa Thurston and Artemas Bishop to Jeremiah Evarts, October 10, 1827, ML, HMCSL.

76. Artemas Bishop to Rufus Anderson, November 3, 1826, ML, HMCSL.

77. Samuel Whitney to Eli Smith, December 27, 1821, ML. Artemas Bishop to Jeremiah Evarts, January 14, 1824, ABCFM-Hawaii Papers, HMCSL.

78. Levi Chamberlain to Jeremiah Evarts, January 8, 1825, ML, HMCSL.

79. Joseph Goodrich to Rufus Anderson, November 11, 1825, Lyman Museum.

80. James Ely to Jeremiah Evarts, November 23, 1826, ML, HMCSL.

81. Levi Chamberlain to Jeremiah Evarts, September 29, 1828, ML, HMCSL.

82. Mercy Whitney to Sarah Bidwell, April 30, 1828, ML, HMCSL.

83. See, Bradley, _The American Frontier in Hawaii_, op. cit.; John Garrett, _To Live Among the Stars: Christian Origins in Oceania_, (Geneva: World Council of Churches, 1982); Aarne A. Koskinen, _Missionary Influence as a Political Factor in the Pacific Islands_, op. cit.; Kuykendall, _The Hawaiian Kingdom_, Vol. I, op. cit.; Chester R. Young, "American Missionary Influence on the Union of Church and State in Hawaii During the Regency of Kaahumanu," _A Journal of Church and State_ IX (1967) 165-179. (Dorton) Kame'eleihiwa, op.cit.

84. Hiram Bingham to Rufus Anderson, December 28, 1828, ML, HMCSL.

85. Bingham, _Residence_, pp. 278-279.

86. Ibid.

87. Ibid., p. 351. (Dorton) Kame'eleihiwa, pp. 195-197, op.cit.

88. Bingham, _Residence_, p. 616.

CHAPTER VI

THE CALL FULFILLED

"These all died in faith, not having received
the promises, but having seen them afar off,
and were persuaded of them, and embraced them,
and confessed that they were strangers and
pilgrims on the earth."   (Hebrews 11:13)

Between 1819 and 1822 twenty-seven dedicated
Christians left Boston for the Sandwich Islands. In the
total missionary effort of Americans and Europeans
during the nineteenth and twentieth centuries, they were
less than a handful. In their interpretation of what
the Great Commission means, they were unique, frozen in
time, trapped in history. Yet, these early missionaries
reveal an explanation of religious faith and cultural
relativism; a mirror of ourselves.

Calvinist theology provided these evangelists with
a bedrock of faith in times of frustration and
disillusionment. "What would the missionary of the
cross do if it were not for the consolation contained in
the promises of God," wrote Samuel Ruggles after two
months in the Sandwich Islands, "these to him are sweet
and refreshing. Without them before him, he would soon
faint and die; but with them he may go to his work and
cheerfully labor and toil" among the Hawaiians. Ruggles
and others in the first two mission companies to Hawai'i
received those promises during the Second Great
Awakening. "When we inquire into the religious history
of those devoted men and women who have gone forth from
the American churches as missionaries to the heathen,"

wrote a contemporary observer, "we generally find, that
the spirit of the enlarged and aspiring enterprise
was cradled in a revival."[1]

Indeed, the revivals of the Second Great Awakening
in New England provided the necessary enthusiasm to make
the cause of foreign missions an American reality.
Students from Andover Theological Seminary provided the
impetus and the initial recruits for the American Board
of Commissioners for Foreign Missions. The missionary
candidates were not complacent in their faith, because
their theology had warned them that only an utterly
selfless love of God brought salvation, yet
disinterested benevolence also compelled them to make
personal sacrifices. The need to serve others caused
the future missionaries to change their lifestyles and
career choices. Levi Chamberlain discovered that his
"conscience was continually urging [him] to go out and
converse with those whom [he] supposed ignorant of the
way of salvation." His partner, Jesse Holbrook, was not
pleased by this turn of events. "I have been
considerably opposed by my partner in reproving profane
persons in the shop -- & distributing tracts." Shortly
thereafter, Chamberlain affiliated with the American
Board to devote himself full time to the Lord's work.
"I do not regret that I relinquished mercantile pursuits
to be engaged in the cause of Missions," Chamberlain
wrote his friend, Rufus Anderson, "nor do I as yet
repent of any one sacrifice that I have ever made for
the Redeemer."[2]

Neither orthodox nor consistent Calvinism, however,
allowed a believer to be totally sure of salvation,
especially if the believer for whatever reason was

unable to participate in a regular quiet time of prayer
and meditation on the Scriptures. The missionaries
often had no free time for prayer and therefore suffered
some mental distress. Betsey Stockton discovered that
although she "always knew that the human heart was a
sink of sin, and that [hers] was filled with it . . .
[she] did not know, until now, that the sink was without
bottom." Her brother missionary Levi Chamberlain
suffered similar feelings of inadequacy. "Never have I
experienced so great a burden of care -- never felt
myself so near sinking under the load imposed upon me."
Charles Stewart, a man of few words concerning his
personal religious experience, was impressed with his
own insignificance before God during a storm at sea. "A
momentary unbelief would persuade me to think myself too
unimportant an object to share in the protecting power"
of God. "All the fortitude of the Christian is
requisite to preserve an ordinary degree of composure,
amidst the terrors of God."[3]

Harriet Stewart's health forced the Stewart
household to return to the United States in 1825. "No
event in my life ever caused me more unfeigned [anxiety]
& distress." Stewart later wrote the mission family at
Honolulu, "it was difficult for me to be reconciled to
a dispensation not only involved in deep darkness
itself, but casting shadows of doubt on the past."[4]

What these shadows were is not known, but they may
have been due to the public expectation that once a
missionary embarked, he or she would not return, unless,
like the Holmans, he or she had not experienced a true
conversion. Foreign missionaries made a lifetime
commitment. To return from the field reflected badly on

both the missionary and the cause, yet fifteen returned
to the United States for reasons of health, including
the Binghams. In some cases the general meeting at
Honolulu was supportive and in some, it was not. It was
a difficult decision. "We are far from thinking it an
easy thing for a missionary to leave his work without
doing injury in some way to the cause of Missions." The
meeting concluded that despite the need to release
missionaries for reasons of health, "we can never assume
the responsibility of justifying any one's quitting the
service or receding from his engagements with the Board
& with the church."[5] Such a conclusion was in keeping
with consistent Calvinism which in theory would question
how an individual could place his or her personal health
above God's call. The tone began to change after the
death of Elizabeth Bishop in 1828. The physical aspects
of Mrs. Bishop's illness were distressing for the
mission family; her spiritual state was frightening.
Levi Chamberlain wrote that "her sufferings were
peculiar and of such a nature as precluded the
consolation usually vouchsafed to those who are truly
the followers of Christ as we have abundant reason to
believe our sister to be." William Richards eulogized
the deceased as "a much loved and useful member of the
mission . . . always more ready to suffer herself than
to see others suffer . . . a mother not only tender but
faithful, -- as a missionary ready to spend and be
spent, -- as a christian had many doubts and fears."
Indeed, "Mr. Bingham told me," Mercy Whitney confided to
Nancy Ruggles, "that [Elizabeth Bishop] warned others
not to live as she had done, in the neglect of duty."[6]

Elizabeth Bishop had perhaps taken contemporary
Calvinism too seriously. While others entertained
doubts for a few moments, hours or even days, Bishop's
doubts permeated her entire Christian life and were
intensified during her last illness. "Her views of the
doctrines & duties of the gospel were clear and
correct," concluded Hiram Bingham, "but she set the
standard of duty so high as hardly to think it possible
that she could be a christian." Bingham suggested
further that Elizabeth's "views of the nature of sin, &
of that holiness, without which no man can see the Lord
were so clear and affecting, that few, on earth, I am
persuaded could entertain the same without deep
solicitude for their own personal safety."[7]

The death, however, though difficult for the
mission family, was conducive to the work. "The loss of
one so endeared to [the Hawaiians]," reported Reverend
Bishop, "the recollection of the many that they had long
neglected her instructions & admonitions until she was
taken from them, and above all, the parting advice she
bequeathed to them as the pledge of her sincerity and
affection aroused them at once to a sense of their
condition." The bereaved missionary reported that "the
idea that [Elizabeth's] dying prayers were offered for
them that they might meet her again in heaven, was a
more powerful appeal to their hearts than all
persuasion." The widower took much comfort in these
events. Perhaps the more so, because they so clearly
fit the Calvinist formula and experience. As Henry
Opukahaia's death brought the missionaries to Hawaii,
Elizabeth Bishop's death brought at least some Hawaiians
to Christ. Such martyrdoms, however, were not to be

encouraged. After the loss of their sister, the remaining missionaries were no longer ambivalent towards medical departures. "If anybody wishes to know the opinion of the brethren on this island about sending home such of our members as have failed in health, I can readily answer that deeply as we feel the loss . . . yet we cannot sacrifice the lives of those who are qualified to be useful . . . merely because the prejudice of many Christians in our own country is against the returning of missionaries."[8]

The greater glory, of course, remained with those who lived out their lives in the missionary field -- at least in the early years. Later, as American and missionary attitudes changed, there was no longer a stigma attached to the worker's return to his or her native land. As the pioneer missionaries became part of an idealized past, the cause of foreign missions fed upon their example. New missionaries were recruited for the Pacific and Asia; new generations looked up to the early nineteenth century examples of Christian life and commitment. William Ellis believed that the early years in the Sandwich Islands had irrefutably proven the benefits of the Christian religion on any nation. "It has afforded fresh encouragements to all interested or engaged in its propagation throughout the world, and has augmented the evidence already possessed, of the adaptation of Christianity to improve the condition of mankind, and its tendency to elevate their intellectual and moral character, and to ameliorate their present condition, whilst it inspires them with the hopes of immortality." Such was the purpose of the first and second company of missionaries to Hawaii, a purpose defined by contemporary Calvinism, individual conversion experiences and a concept of the missionary calling formed by past experience and contemporary ideals. Charles Stewart reflected the feelings of the entire missionary family when he wrote, "It is with emotions of gratitude to God, that he has not only given me . . . a good hope through grace of his great laboration. And called me by his Spirit into the ministry of His Son. But, that He has also disposed my heart to devote myself to the building up of his Kingdom in the Pagan world."[9]

THE CALL FULFILLED - ENDNOTES

1. Samuel and Nancy Ruggles, May 8, 1820, Journal, JC, HMCSL. Calvin Colton, *History and Character of American Revivals*, (1832; reprint, New York: AMS Press, 1973), pp. 194-195.

2. Levi Chamberlain, March 6, 1820, Journal, JC; to Rufus Anderson, November 20, 1822, ML, HMCSL.

3. *Christian Advocate*, December 1824, p. 564. Levi Chamberlain to Jeremiah Evarts, January 9, 1824, ML, HMCSL. Stewart, *Journal*, op. cit., pp. 40-41.

4. Charles Stewart to Missionaries Resident at the Sandwich Islands, November 20, 1829, ML, HMCSL.

5. Joint Letter of the Sandwich Islands Mission to the American Board, October 7, 1826, ABCFM-HEA Papers, HMCSL.

6. Levi Chamberlain, March 3, 1828, Journal, JC. William Richards to Jeremiah Evarts, April 14, 1828, ABCFM-Hawaii Papers. Mercy Whitney to Nancy Ruggles, April 2, 1828, ML, HMCSL.

7. Hiram Bingham to Jeremiah Evarts, March 12, 1828, ML, HMCSL.

8. Artemas Bishop to Jeremiah Evarts, January 3, 1828; to Levi Chamberlain, September 13, 1828, ML, HMCSL.

9. Stewart, *Journal*, op. cit., p. xv; Letters of Candidacy, ML, HMCSL.

APPENDIX A

MISSIONARY PROFILES

THE REVEREND HIRAM BINGHAM

Born: October 30, 1789 at Bennington, Vermont
Died: November 11, 1869 at New Haven, Connecticut
Education: Middlebury College (1816)
            Andover Theological Seminary (1819)
First Company

While enroute to his mission station, Hiram Bingham
reassured his parents. "You may while you live & even
in your dying bed derive comfort from the reflection that
in training up a numerous family for God, he has enabled
you to do something towards preparing one missionary of
the cross for the destitute at home and another for
perishing pagans abroad."[1]

MRS. SYBIL MOSELEY BINGHAM

Born: September 14, 1792 at Westfield, Massachusetts
Died: February 17, 1848 at Easthampton, Massachusetts
First Company

On her wedding day the new Mrs. Bingham confided to her
journal, "I pen this date, and pause. Happy day! that
joined me to the worthiest of husbands -- that opened the
way, plain & wide, into missionary work."[2]

THE REVEREND ARTEMAS BISHOP

Born: December 30, 1795 at Pompey, New York
Died: December 18, 1872 at Honolulu, Hawai'i
Education: Union College (1819)
            Princeton Theological Seminary (1822)
Second Company

Enroute to the Sandwich Islands, Bishop reflected that,
"So much of a pilgrim have I become that the distance of
time which separates Eternity from my view seems very
short; and the thought of meeting my friends there quite

familiar. Much of the dread of Death, which I used to feel, is taken away in the joyful hope of greeting . . . those whom I leave here on earth."[3]

MRS. ELIZABETH EDWARDS BISHOP

Born: June 2, 1798 at Marlborough, Massachusetts
Died: February 21, 1828 at Kailua-Kona, Hawai'i
Education: Bradford Academy
Second Company

Mrs. Bishop shared some of her religious anxiety with Mrs. Louisa Ely. "Poor, weak nature trembles and faints in view of approaching trials. But all I ask is a soul truly resigned and submissive to all which my Father shall appoint. This is the burden of my prayer, and the one blessing for which I dare to look with confidence."[4]

DR. ABRAHAM BLATCHELY

Born: October 13, 1787 at East Guilford (Madison),
          Connecticut
Died: 1860 in Illinois
Education: Yale College
Second Company

Dr. Blatchely was never contented in Hawaii, and what little documentation he left is usually of a complaining nature. Dr. Blatchley left the mission station in 1826 for health reasons. "The climate is more debilitating than I expected," he wrote, "I have at no time been able to do but little, have been subject to frequent bilious affections which have as frequently prostrated my strength, & have at times been laid low by the fever of a tropical climate."[5]

MRS. JEMIMA MARVIN BLATCHELY

Born: March 28, 1791 at Lyme, Connecticut
Died: October 26, 1856 at East Guilford, Connecticut
Second Company

After returning to the United States, Mrs. Blatchely wrote Mrs. Nancy Ruggles, "how sad . . . is the feeling that I can no more be associated with those who are engaged in spreading the Gospel among benighted pagans, tho' at the same time I am overwhelmed with a consciousness of my own unworthiness . . . in such a service."[6]

MR. DANIEL CHAMBERLAIN

Born: March 11, 1782 at Westboro, Massachusetts
Died: February 6, 1860 at Westboro, Massachusetts
Occupation: Farmer
First Company

As the Chamberlains prepared for their departure from the Sandwich Islands Daniel Chamberlain expressed his disappointment. "But dear brethren the thoughts of leaving you -- of leaving the work which I would desire with my whole soul still to aid -- brings to mind a trail of tender feelings which my feeble pen cannot express -- cannot paint!"[7]

MRS. JERUSHA BURNAP CHAMBERLAIN

Born: November 19, 1786 at Hopkinton, Massachusetts
Died: June 27, 1879 at Wollaston, Massachusetts
First Company

Jerusha Chamberlain left no known writings. In a letter to Jeremiah Evarts, Daniel Chamberlain noted that, "Mrs. C sends her love to Mrs. Evarts & wishes to be remembered to all enquiring friends -- She says she has not regretted for a moment her undertaking since she left America."[8]

MR. LEVI CHAMBERLAIN

Born: August 28, 1792 at Dover, Vermont
Died: July 29, 1849 at Honolulu, Hawai'i
Occupation: Accountant and Superintendent for Secular
            Affairs
Second Company

According to Levi Chamberlain "Christian contentment . . . is complacency in the divine dispensations, and satisfaction with the allotments of providence, -- heathen contentment is that of the sevine [sic], exercised without thought, and upon a sated appetite."[9]

MR. JAMES ELY

Born: October 22, 1798 at Lyme, Connecticut
Died: January 20, 1890 at Thompsonville, Connecticut
Education: Foreign Mission School
Occupation: Licensed Preacher
           Ordained at Honolulu, Hawai'i; June 4, 1825
Second Company

"It was early my desire to be a missionary. And I think I was influenced in my decisions on this subject more from a sense of duty than from flattering prospects of care or preferment." Indeed, "I nearly despaired of doing anything for Christ. But since I have resided at Kaawaloa, God has been better to me than my fears. My service rendered has been cheerful, and I have experienced real satisfaction in making known the way of life."[10]

MRS. LOUISA EVEREST ELY

Born: September 8, 1793 at Cornwell, Connecticut
Died: September 15, 1848 at Cornwell, Connecticut
Second Company

"There on the black rocks of Kaawaloa, I spent some of the happiest moments of my life."[11]

MR. JOSEPH GOODRICH

Born: July 31, 1794 at Wethersfield, Connecticut
Died: February 19, 1852 at Kewanee, Illinois
Education: Yale College
Occupation: Licensed Preacher
           Ordained September 29, 1826; Kailua-Kona,
           Hawai'i
Second Company

Levi Chamberlain requested Goodrich to indicate his needs. "My wants are great. The first, great, and main is some one to take part with me in the ministry of reconciliation to assist in counseling these poor heathen who are constantly enquiring at our hands the way of life."[12]

MRS. MARTHA BARNES GOODRICH

Born: January 8, 1801 at Southington, Connecticut
Died: November 6, 1840 at Kewanee, Illinois
Second Company

Homesickness afflicted all of the missionaries. Mrs. Goodrich confided, "Often when I think of you, it is vain that I endeavour to suppress the rising sigh, and falling tear.   But I think not that it is because I am discontented and wish to return, for I am far generally happier than I deserve to be, but when I think of home, a thousand tender recollections rush into my mind, and I for a moment indulge the tears to flow silently down my cheek."[13]

DR. THOMAS HOLMAN

Born: November 26, 1793 at New Haven, Connecticut
Died: March 20, 1826 at Bridgeport, Connecticut
Education: Cherry Valley Medical School, New York
             Foreign Mission School
First Company

From the day the Thaddeus set sail the Holmans were under a cloud.   "The fact is," Daniel Chamberlain wrote, "I believe & I have good reason for my belief -- that it was their intention to come here & stay a few years & accumulate some property & then return."[14]

MRS. LUCIA RUGGLES HOLMAN

Born: October 12, 1793 at Brookfield, Connecticut
Died: June 20, 1886 at New Milford, Connecticut
First Company

Soon after the arrival of the Thaddeus, "one of the queens, weighing at least 350, got me into her lap, & felt me from heat to foot & said I must eat more to grow larger.   She wanted me to take my hair down to see how long it was & then how I roll it up."[15]

MR. ELISHA LOOMIS

Born: December 11, 1799 at Rushville, New York
Died: August 27, 1836 at Rushville, New York

Education: Foreign Mission School
Occupation: Printer, Teacher
First Company

While under conviction, Mr. Loomis exclaimed, "When I
look into myself I perceive scarcely anything but sin .
. . . Blessed Jesus! deliver me from the power of sin and
satan."[16]

MRS. MARIA THERESA SARTWELL LOOMIS

Born: August 25, 1796 at Hartford, New York
Died: September 6, 1862 at Ypsilanti, Michigan
First Company

The women were distracted from their missionary work by
family concerns, but occasionally the two coincided.
"Yesterday I was permitted the high privilege of
presenting to God in the holy ordinance of baptism, my
precious little babe [Amanda], & of renewedly dedicating
myself, my offspring & my all to his service."[17]

THE REVEREND WILLIAM RICHARDS

Born: August 22, 1793 at Plainfield, Massachusetts
Died: November 7, 1847 at Honolulu, Hawai'i
Education: Williams College (1819)
            Andover Theological Seminary (1822)
Second Company

In the 1828 Report of Mission co-authored by William
Richards and Lorrin Andrews the statement was made that
"when we speak of what we have done, we ought to be
ashamed of our moral, religious and official characters,
as falling short of our engagements and your
requisitions." Nevertheless, "with all our weakness and
imperfections, we verily believe that God has glorified
himself in bringing by our instrumentality some souls out
of darkness into his marvelous light."[18]

MRS. CLARISSA LYMAN RICHARDS

Born: January 10, 1795 at Northampton, Massachusetts
Died: October 3, 1861 at New Haven, Connecticut
Second Company

William Richards recounted an incident when the female chief, Thekawenoke, told Clarissa Richards to make her three gowns, because it was less trouble for the missionary to make them than for the chief's attendants. Mrs. Richards responded that "I am now here alone in feeble health -- I make my own clothes, the clothes of my family, & have no girls to assist me in it -- I have not a company of servants about me to go and come at my bidding & do all my work, but must do really all my working and much of my other work myself -- I have a number of scholars to teach everyday -- I have made you three gowns, and taught your girls to sew." The chief left in a huff.[19]

MR. SAMUEL RUGGLES

Born: March 9, 1795 at Brookfield, Connecticut
Died: September 6, 1871 at Fort Atkinson, Wisconsin
Education: Foreign Mission School
Occupation: Teacher/Catechist
First Company

Prior to his departure for Hawai'i, Samuel Ruggles confided to his sister, Lucia, "The idea of going is sometimes for a moment almost insupportable, but when I think of the vast worth of souls, and the glorious cause which . . . I go to promote, all disagreeable sensations vanish."[20]

MRS. NANCY WELLS RUGGLES

Born: April 12, 1791 at East Windsor, Connecticut
Died: February 28, 1873 at Fort Atkinson, Wisconsin
First Company

"The idea of being left a wanderer as it were alone, in a strange land, is very trying; but I will not murmur; the Lord afflicts not willingly."[21]

THE REVEREND CHARLES SAMUEL STEWART

Born: October 16, 1795 at Flemington, New Jersey
Died: December 14, 1870 at Cooperstown, New York
Education: Princeton College (1815)
           Princeton Theological Seminary (1821)
Second Company

After the departure of Lord Byron in 1825, Charles
Stewart reflected, "Nothing I have yet known on
Missionary ground, causes me so deeply to feel the
sacrifice of our situation, as the occasional society of
such men. The lowliness of our habitation, the plainness
and poverty of our table, the known and unknown
inconveniences and privations of our establishment --
never rouse the recollections of mind and heart, excited
by the intercourse of a week, a day, an hour, with the
polished, the intelligent, the amiable, the virtuous."[22]

MRS. HARRIET BRADFORD TIFFANY STEWART

Born: June 24, 1798 at Stamford, Connecticut
Died: September 6, 1830 at Cooperstown, New York
Second Company

Always in poor health, Harriet Stewart nearly died in
1825 after the birth of her daughter, Harriet. The
Reverend Stewart confided, after the danger was past,
that at her darkest hour the sick woman's friends "had
the highest consolation of seeing imparted to her, by her
covenant with God, not only a spirit of resignation and
peace, but thoughts of brightness and of joy, from a good
hope through grace of entering on 'the rest that
remaineth to his people.'"[23]

MISS BETSEY STOCKTON

Born: c. 1798 at Princeton, New Jersey
Died: October 24, 1865 at Princeton, New Jersey
Occupation: Teacher
Second Company

"A missionary's life is very laborous but pleasant."[24]

THE REVEREND ASA THURSTON

Born: October 12, 1787 at Firchburg, Massachusetts
Died: March 11, 1868 at Honolulu, Hawai'i
Education: Yale College (1816)
            Andover Theological Seminary (1819)
First Company

To the despair of the missionaries Liholiho (Kamehameha II) did not express much interest in the new religion. Nevertheless, they were "not without hope that [Liholiho] will sometime exchange his rum bottle for his bible."[25]

MRS. LUCY GOODALE THURSTON

Born: October 29, 1795 at Marlborough, Massachusetts
Died: October 13, 1876 at Honolulu, Hawai'i
Education: Bradford Academy
First Company

The Thurstons served at Kailua-Kona alone after the departure of the Holmans. "Having no protection whatever against the admission of evil, I stood in my lot, strengthening myself to the inglorious work of looking after the stuff, while my husband looked after the people; and the angels looked after me."[26]

MR. SAMUEL WHITNEY

Born: April 28, 1793 at Branford, Connecticut
Died: December 15, 1845 at Lahainaluna, Maui, Hawaii
Education: Yale College
Occupation: Teacher
          Ordained at Kailua, Hawai'i; November 23, 1825
First Company

The missionaries often experienced a spiritual draining due in part to their isolation from regular Christian fellowship and also to the general fatigue of their labors. Samuel Whitney shared his spiritual emptiness with Levi Chamberlain. "I am pained to hear you complain of spiritual languor in your own heart, and wish I could say it were otherwise with me; but heart religion with me is very low, and I fear the ebb."[27]

MRS. MERCY PARTRIDGE WHITNEY

Born: August 14, 1795 at Pittsfield, Massachusetts
Died: December 26, 1872 at Waimea, Kaua'i, Hawai'i
First Company

It was with great personal anguish that many missionary parents decided to send their children back to the United

States where they could receive an education free from
island influences. "While Maria was with us, she was
considerable company for me; but shall I say she has
gone, & I expect to see her no more on earth?   The
thought indeed pains me; but still I cannot wish her
back." The hearts of the bereft parents "still cling to
her as the object of our affection & solicitude. Nothing
but a sense of duty which we owe the child, could
reconcile us to the separation."[28]

MISSIONARY PROFILES - ENDNOTES

1. Hiram Bingham to Calvin Bingham, February 26, 1819, Bingham Family Papers, Box 1, Folder 1, HMCSL. All material relating to birth and death dates and locations, and education taken from the Missionary Album, op. cit. unless otherwise noted.

2. Sybil Bingham, October 11, 1822, Journal, JC, HMCSL.

3. Artemas Bishop to an unknown woman in New York, December 20, 1822, ABCFM-Hawaii, HMCSL.

4. Elizabeth Bishop to Louisa Ely, January 13, 1825, ML, HMCSL.

5. John Andrew indicates that Dr. Blatchely did not attend college, but had attended two lecture courses at a medical school in New Haven, Connecticut. See Andrew, p. 132. Abraham Blatchely to Jeremiah Evarts, July 26, 1826, ML, HMCSL.

6. Jemima Blatchely to Nancy Ruggles, December 4, 1828, ML, HMCSL.

7. Daniel and Jerusha Chamberlain to the Pastors and Brethren of the Church of the Sandwich Islands Mission, March 7, 1823, ML, HMCSL.

8. Daniel Chamberlain to Jeremiah Evarts, October 6, 1820, ML, HMCSL.

9. Levi Chamberlain to Rufus Anderson, February 13, 1827, ML, HMCSL.

10. James Ely to Levi Chamberlain, October 3, 1825, ML, HMCSL.

11. Louisa Ely to Maria Chamberlain, October 24, 1831, ML, HMCSL.

12. Joseph Goodrich to Levi Chamberlain, December 21, 1829, Lyman Museum.

13. Martha Goodrich, March 29, 1823, Journal, JC, HMCSL.

14. Daniel Chamberlain to Samuel Worcester, November 14, 1820, ML, HMCSL.

15. Lucia Holman, March, 1820, Journal, op. cit.

16. Elisha Loomis to Joseph Webb, n.d. (during the years 1816-1817), ML, HMCSL.

17. Maria Loomis to Nancy Ruggles, February 17, 1822, ML, HMCSL.

18. Lorrin Andrews and William Richards to Jeremiah Evarts, Report of the Mission, September 30, 1828, ABCFM-Houghton, HMCSL.

19. William Richards to Jeremiah Evarts, June 1, 1824, ABCFM-Houghton, HMCSL.

20. Samuel Ruggles to Lucia Ruggles (Holman), July 2, 1817, ML, HMCSL.

21. Samuel and Nancy Ruggles, November 6, 1819, Journal, JC, HMCSL.

22. Charles Stewart, May 26, 1825, Journal, op. cit.

23. Ibid., April 19, 1825.

24. Christian Advocate, May 1824, p. 232.

25. Asa Thurston to Samuel Worcester, May 4, 1821, ML, HMCSL.

26. L. Thurston, Life, op. cit., pp. 58-59.

27. Samuel Whitney to Levi Chamberlain, December 21, 1826, ML, HMCSL.

28. Mercy Whitney to Elizabeth Bishop, December 11, 1826, ML, HMCSL.

APPENDIX B

STATISTICS

It is difficult to derive meaningful statistics from such a small sample. However, there are some interesting facts concerning the ages of the missionaries when they departed for Hawai'i and their length of service in the field.[1]

I. Ages at Departure

It is generally thought that the missionaries in the first two companies were young married couples. In fact, the majority of departing missionaries were over the age of twenty-five. It should be noted, however, that while the years twenty-five to thirty are presently viewed as belonging to the more mature young adult years, such was not the case in the early nineteenth century when a man was not considered settled until he was at least thirty and married.[2] "Youth," then becomes a relative term.

TABLE 1

Ages at Departure

Name	Age	Date of Birth
First Company		
H. Bingham	30	1789
S. Bingham	27	1792
D. Chamberlain	37	1782
J. Chamberlain	33	1786
T. Holman	26	1793
L. Holman	26	1793
E. Loomis	20	1799
M. Loomis	23	1796
S. Ruggles	24	1795
N. Ruggles	28	1791
A. Thurston	32	1787
L. Thurston	24	1795
S. Whitney	26	1793
M. Whitney	24	1795
Second Company		
A. Bishop	28	1795
E. Bishop	25	1798
A. Blatchely	36	1787
J. Blatchely	32	1791
L. Chamberlain	31	1792
J. Ely	25	1798
L. Ely	30	1793
J. Goodrich	29	1794
M. Goodrich	22	1801
W. Richards	30	1793
C. Richards	28	1795
C. Stewart	28	1795
H. Stewart	25	1798
B. Stockton	25	1798

TABLE 2

Ages at Departure

20-25	26-30	30+
10	12	28

As indicated by Tables 1 and 2, of the twenty-eight departing missionaries under consideration only 35.8 per cent were twenty-five and under. Fully 42.8 per cent were in the mid-range of twenty-six to thirty, and 21.4 per cent were over the age of thirty. This changes the picture of these missionaries from that of young and inexperienced persons to one of possibly immature individuals who may have been ignorant of their destination, but were of an age when they might be expected to know their own minds.

It would be interesting to know the dates when these individuals experienced conversion and determined to accept the call to mission. It may be that the career choice was made at a much earlier age (as is indicated by some of the testimony previously presented). The departure date would then be the first opportunity of implementing an existing commitment.

II. Length of Service

The majority of those leaving the field did so within the first three to five years for health related reasons (36.6 per cent). Using a base of thirty to include Delia Stone Bishop and Maria Patton Chamberlain, 43 per cent of the individuals embarking on the mission left the field before 1830 and 23 per cent left after 1830. Only 33.3 per cent remained in Hawai'i until their respective deaths.

Five individuals returned to the United States for non-health related reasons. Dr. and Mrs. Thomas Holman were excommunicated. Mr. and Mrs. Joseph Goodrich left after disagreements with the American Board and the mission family over Mr. Goodrich's participation in apparent economic activities. Mrs. Clarissa Richards returned in 1849 after being widowed two years previously. William Richards died in Hawai'i, but had been released by the American Board in 1838 in order to become an advisor to Kamehameha III. The former missionary also served as ambassador to Great Britain and Minister of Public Instruction.

TABLE 3
Departures from the Field

Name	Dates of Service	Reasons for Departure	Release
Prior to 1830			
A. Blatchely	1823-1826	health	1827
J. Blatchely			
D. Chamberlain	1820-1823	health/education	1823
J. Chamberlain		of children	
J. Ely	1823-1828	health	1830
L. Ely		health	
T. Holman	1820-1821	excommunication	1822
L. Holman		censure	
E. Loomis	1820-1827	health	---
M. Loomis			
C. Stewart	1823-1825		1830
H. Stewart		health	
B. Stockton	1823-1825	H. Stewart's health	

Name	Dates of Service	Reasons for Departure	Release

After 1830

Name	Dates of Service	Reasons for Departure	Release
H. Bingham	1820-1840		1846
S. Bingham		health	
J. Goodrich	1823-1836	conflict of interest	1836
M. Goodrich			
C. Richards	1823-1838/1849	widowed 1847	1838
S. Ruggles	1820-1834	health	1836
N. Ruggles			

TABLE 4

Deaths in the Field

Name	Arrival Date		Date of Death
A. Bishop	1823		1872
E. Bishop	1823		1828
D. Bishop	1828		1875
L. Chamberlain	1823		1849
M. Chamberlain	1828		1880
A. Thurston	1820		1868
L. Thurston	1820		1876
S. Whitney	1820		1845
M. Whitney	1820		1872
W. Richards	1823	released 1838	1847

TABLE 5

Years in the Field

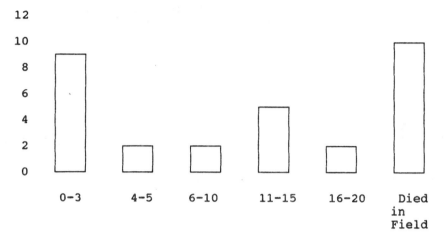

Those remaining less than three years: Dr. Abraham
Blatchely, Mrs. Jemima Blatchely, Mr. Daniel Chamberlain,
Mrs. Jerusha Chamberlain, Dr. Thomas Holman, Mrs. Lucia
Holman, Rev. Charles Stewart, Mrs. Harriet Stewart, Miss
Betsey Stockton.

Those remaining four to five years: Mr. James Ely, Mrs.
Louisa Ely.

Those remaining six to ten years: Mr. Elisha Loomis,
Mrs. Maria Loomis.

Those remaining eleven to fifteen years: Mr. Joseph
Goodrich, Mrs. Martha Goodrich, Rev. William Richards
[resigned but stayed in the islands], Mrs. Clarissa
Richards [resigned but stayed in the islands], Mr. Samuel
Ruggles, Mrs. Nancy Ruggles.

Those remaining sixteen to twenty years: Rev. Hiram
Bingham, Mrs. Sybil Bingham.

Those who died in the field: Rev. Artemas Bishop, Mrs.
Elizabeth Bishop, (Mrs. Delia Bishop), Mr. Levi

Chamberlain, {Mrs. Maria Chamberlain}, Rev. Asa Thurston, Mrs. Lucy Thurston, Mr. Samuel Whitney, Mrs. Mercy Whitney.

Names in enclosures [{}] are members of the Third Company (1828) who married earlier missionaries.

Half of the missionaries returned to the United States for health related reasons affecting one or both spouses. Inasmuch as health was the only acceptable reason for a return from the mission field, there were undoubtedly cases where it was used as an excuse by those who had second thoughts.

STATISTICS - ENDNOTES

1. Raw figures for statistical data taken from Bernice Judd, Advisor, Missionary Album (Honolulu HI: Hawaiian Mission Children's Society, 1969).

2. See Lois Banner, "Religion and Reform in the Early Republic: The Role of Youth," American Quarterly, 23 (1971) : 677-695.

SELECTED BIBLIOGRAPHY

Manuscript Collections

From the Hawaiian Mission Children's Society Library, Honolulu, Hawaii:

ABCFM-HEA Papers

ABCFM-Hawaii Papers, Houghton Library (Harvard)

Bingham Family Papers

The Journal Collection

Letters of Candidacy

Missionary Letters

From the Hawaiian Historical Society, Honolulu, Hawaii:

Donald Angus Typed Manuscripts

From the Kathryn E. Lyle Memorial Library, Lyman House Memorial Museum, Hilo, Hawaii:

Goodrich Letters

Primary Sources

ABCFM. Instructions to the Missionaries about to embark for the Sandwich Islands; and to the Rev. Mssrs. William Goodell, and Isaac Bird, Attached to the Palestine Mission. Boston: Crocker and Brewster. 1823.

ABCFM. Memorial Volume of the First Fifty Years of the American Board of Commissioners for Foreign Missions. Boston: American Board of Commissioners for Foreign Missions. 1861.

ABCFM. Narrative of Five Youth from the Sandwich Islands, now receiving an Education in this Country. New York: J. Seymour. 1816.

Allen, Jonathan. A Sermon Delivered at Haverhill, February 5, 1812 on the occasion of the young ladies about to embark as the wives of Rev. Messieurs Judson and Newell, going as Missionaries to India. In R. Pierce Beaver, ed. Pioneers in Mission. Grand Rapids MI: William B. Eerdmans Publishing Company. 1966. 268-278.

Bartlett, Samuel C. Historical Sketch of the Missions of the American Board in the Sandwich Islands, Micronesia and Marquesas. 1876. Reprint, New York: Arno Press. 1972.

Beecher, Lyman. The Faith Once Delivered to the Saints. In William G. McLoughlan, ed. The American Evangelicals 1800-1900. New York: Harper & Row, Publishers. 1968. 70-85.

Beecher, Lyman. Views of Theology. Cincinnati: Truman and Smith. 1836.

Bingham, Hiram. A Residence of Twenty-one Years in the Sandwich Islands. 1849. Reprint, Rutland VT: Charles E. Tuttle Company. 1981.

Bogue, David. Objections against a mission to the heathen, stated and considered. Cambridge, England: Hilliard and Metcalf. 1811.

Brainerd, David. Memoirs. In Stephen Nissenbaum, ed. The Great Awakening at Yale College. Belmont CA: Wadsworth Publishing Company, Inc. 1976. 37-51.

Branagan, Thomas. The Excellency of the Female Character Vindicated. 1808. Reprint, New York: Arno Press. 1972.

Christian Advocate. (Philadelphia). 1823-1825.

Colton, Calvin, Rev. History and Character of American Revivals. 1832. Reprint, New York: AMS Press. 1973.

Cross, Barbara M. ed. The Autobiography of Lyman Beecher. Vol. 1. Cambridge MA: The Belknap Press of Harvard University Press. 1961.

Dwight, Edwin. Memoirs of Henry Obookiah. 1818. Reprint, Honolulu: Women's Board of Missions for the Pacific Islands. 1968.

Dwight, Timothy. Theology: Explained and Defended. Vol. 1-4. New Haven: T. Dwight & Son. 1839.

Eddy, Daniel C. Daughters of the Cross. New York: Doyton and Wentworth. 1855.

Edwards, Jonathan. Distinguishing Marks of a Work of the Spirit of God. In Nissenbaum. op. cit.

Edwards, Jonathan. The Life of Rev. David Brainerd. New York: American Tract Society. n.d.

Edwards, Jonathan. Thoughts on the Revival of Religion in New England and the Way in which it Ought to be Acknowledged and Promoted. Northampton MA: Simeon Butler. 1819.

Ellis, William. The American Mission in the Sandwich Islands, a Vindication and an Appeal to the Proceedings of the Reformed Catholic Mission at Honolulu. Honolulu: H. M. Whitney. 1866.

Ellis, William. ed. The Christian Keepsake and Missionary Annual. London: Fisher, Son & Co. 1838.

Gallaudet, Thomas H. An Address delivered at a Meeting for Prayer with reference to the Sandwich Mission in the Birch Church in Hartford, October 11, 1819. Hartford CT: Lincoln & Stone, Printers. 1819.

Gisborne, Thomas. An Enquiry into the Duties of the Female Sex. London: A. Strahan. 1801.

Hopkins, Samuel. A Treatise on the Millennium. In Gordon S. Wood, ed. The Rising Glory of America 1760-1820. New York: George Braziller. 1971.

Holman, Lucia Ruggles. Journal. Honolulu: Bishop Museum Special Publications No. 17. 1931.

Humphrey, Heman. The Promised Land, a Sermon delivered at Goshen (Conn.) at the Ordination of the Rev. Mssrs. Hiram Bingham & Asa Thurston as Missionaries to the Sandwich Islands, Sept. 29, 1819. Boston: Samuel T. Armstrong. 1819.

Morse, Jedediah; Worcester, Samuel; and Evarts, Jeremiah. "Address to the Christian Public." Second through Fourth Annual Meetings. First Ten Annual Meetings of the ABCFM. Boston: Crocker and Brewster. 1834.

Prime, E. D. G. Forty Years in the Turkish Empire. Boston: American Board of Commissioners for Foreign Missions. 1891.

Panoplist/Missionary Herald (Boston). Vol. 1-19. 1805-1823.

Stewart, Charles S. Journal of a Residence in the Sandwich Islands 1823-1825. 1830. Reprint, Honolulu: University of Hawaii Press. 1970.

Strebeck, George. A Sermon on the Character of the Virtuous Woman. New York. 1800.

Thompson, Charles L. Times of Refreshing, A History of American Revivals from 1740-1877. Chicago: M. W. Smith & Co. 1877.

Thurston, Lucy Goodale. Life and Times of Lucy G. Thurston. 1882. Reprint, Honolulu: The Friend. 1934.

Tracy, Joseph. The Great Awakening. 1845. Reprint, New York: Arno Press. 1969.

Tracy, Joseph. "History of the American Board of Commissioners for Foreign Missions." In History of American Missions to the Heathen from their Commencement to the Present Time. Worcester MA: Spooner & Howland. 1840.

Wadsworth, Benjamin. The Well-Ordered Family or Relative Duties Being the Substance of Several Sermons. Boston: Printed by B. Green for Nicholas Battolph. 1712.

Woods, Leonard. A Sermon Delivered at the Tabernacle in Salem, Feb. 6, 1812, on the Occasion of the Ordination of the Rev. Messrs. Samuel Newell, A. M.; Adoniram Judson, A. M.; Samuel Nott, A. M.; Gordon Hall, A. M.; and Luther Rice, A. B.; Missionaries

to the Heathen in Asia Under the direction of the
[American] Board of Commissioners for Foreign
Missions. In R. Pierce Beaver, ed. Pioneers. op.
cit. 257-268.

Worcester, Samuel. Mission to the Sandwich Islands.
Boston: U. Crocker, Printer. 1819.

Worcester, Samuel. "Instructions Given by the Prudential
Committee of the ABCFM, to the Missionaries to the
East, February 7, 1812." Third Annual Meeting. First
Ten Annual Meetings. op. cit.

Secondary Sources - Unpublished

Banner, Lois Wendland. "The Protestant Crusade: Religious
Missions, Benevolence, and Reform in the United
States, 1790-1840." Ph.D. dissertation, Columbia
University, 1970.

Bingham, Hiram, III. "Notes on the Life of Hiram
Bingham." Ph.D. dissertation, Yale University, 1949.

Burlingham, Katherine Louise. "The Necessity of Sound
Doctrine: A Study of Calvinism and its Opponents as
Seen in American Religious Periodicals 1800-1815."
Ph.D. dissertation, University of Oregon, 1965.

Caskey, Marie Carpenter. "Faith and Theology in the
Beecher Family." Ph.D. dissertation, Yale
University, 1974.

Constantine, Charles Joseph. "The New Divinity Men."
Ph.D. dissertation, University of California at
Berkeley, 1972.

Della Vecchia, Phyllis Ann. "Rhetoric, Religion,
Politics: A Study of the Sermons of Lyman Beecher."
Ph.D. dissertation, University of Pennsylvania,
1973.

(Dorton) Kame'eleihiwa, Lilikala. "Land and the Promise
of Capitalism: A Dilemma for the Hawaiian Chiefs of
the 1848 Mahele." Ph.D. dissertation, University of
Hawaii at Manoa, 1986.

Easton, Barbara Leslie. "Women, Religion and the Family: Revivalism as an Indicator of Social Change in Early New England." Ph.D. dissertation, University of California at Berkeley, 1975.

Grimshaw, Patricia. "Paths of Duty: American Missionary Wives in the Early Nineteenth Century." Ph.D. dissertation, University of Melbourne, 1986.

Hart, Sidney. "The American Sense of Mission, 1783-1810: Puritan Historical Myths in Post-Revolutionary New England." Ph.D. dissertation, Clark University, 1973.

Lloyd, Peter. "The Emergence of a Racial Prejudice Towards the Indians in Seventeenth Century New England: Some Notes on an Explanation." Ph.D. dissertation, Ohio State University, 1975.

Perry, Alan Frederick. "The American Board of Commissioners for Foreign Missions and the London Missionary Society in the Nineteenth Century: A Study of Ideas." Ph.D. dissertation, Washington University, 1974.

Rabinowitz, Richard I. "Soul, Character, and Personality: The Transformation of Personal Religious Experience in New England, 1790-1860." Ph.D. dissertation, Harvard University, 1977.

Salisbury, Neal Emerson. "Conquest of the "Savage" : Puritans, Puritan Missionaries, and Indians 1620-1680." Ph.D. dissertation, University of California at Los Angeles, 1972.

Shiels, Richard Douglas. "The Connecticut Clergy in the Second Great Awakening." Ph.D. dissertation, Boston University Graduate School, 1976.

Vos, Howard Frederick. "The Great Awakening in Connecticut.," Ph.D. dissertation, Northwestern University, 1967.

Secondary Sources - Articles

"Sketch of the life, labors and death of the Rev. Samuel Whitney, 25 years a missionary of the ABCFM Missions at the Sandwich Islands." The Friend, Jan. 15, 1846.

Andrew, John A., III. "Betsey Stockton: Stranger in a Strange Land." Journal of Presbyterian History. 52 (Summer, 1974) : 157-166.

Banner, Lois. "Religion and Reform in the Early Republic: The Role of Youth." American Quarterly. 23 (1971) : 677-695.

Barrere, Dorothy and Sahlins, Marshall. "Tahitians in the early history of Hawaiian Christianity: The Journal of Toketa." Hawaiian Journal of History. 13 (1979) : 19-35.

Beaver, R. Pierce. "Methods of American Missions to the Indians in the Seventeenth and Eighteenth Centuries: Calvinist Models for Protestant Foreign Missions." Journal of Presbyterian History. 47 (1969) : 124-148.

Bingham, Alfred M. "Sybil's Bones, A Chronicle of the Three Hiram Binghams." Hawaiian Journal of History. 9 (1975) : 3-36.

Birdsall, Richard D. "The Second Great Awakening and the New England Social Order." Church History. (1970) : 345-364.

Blauvelt, Martha Tomhave and Keller, Rosemary Skinner. "Women and Revivalism: The Puritan and Weslyan Traditions." Women and Religion in America. Vol. 2. Reuther, Rosemary Radford and Keller, Rosemary Skinner, eds. San Francisco: Harper & Row Publishers. 1981. 316-367.

Blight, James G. "Jonathan Edwards' Theory of the Mind: Its Applications and Implications." Explorations in the History of Psychology in the United States. Brozek, Josef, ed. Cranbury NJ: Associated University Presses Inc. 1984.

Brown, G. Gordon. "Missionaries and Cultural Diffusion." American Journal of Sociology. L (1944) : 214-219.

Carothers, J. C. "Culture, Psychiatry and the Written Word." Psychiatry. XXII (1959) : 307-320.

Conforti, Joseph A. "Samuel Hopkins and the New Divinity: Theology, Ethics and Social Reform in Eighteenth Century New England." William and Mary Quarterly. 37 (1977) : 572-589.

Cott, Nancy F. "Young Women in the Second Great Awakening in New England." Feminist Studies. 3 (1975) : 15-29.

Dodd, Carol S. "Betsey Stockton: A History Student's Perspective." Educational Perspectives. 16 (1977) : 10-15.

Elliott, Emory. "The Dove and Serpent: The Clergy in the American Revolution." American Quarterly. XXXI (1979) : 187-203.

Elsbree, Oliver Wendell. "Samuel Hopkins and His Doctrine of Benevolence." New England Quarterly. VIII (1935) : 534-550.

Erikson, Erik H. "Psychological Reality and Historical Actuality." Insight and Responsibility. Erikson, Erik H., ed., New York: W. W. Norton and Company. 1964. 159-216.

Good, L. Douglas. "The Christian Nation in the Mind of Timothy Dwight." Fides et Historia. 7 (1974) : 1-18.

Grimshaw, Patricia. "Christian Woman, Pious Wife, Faithful Mother, Devoted Missionary: Conflicts in Roles of American Missionary Women in Nineteenth Century Hawaii." Feminist Studies. 9 (1983) : 489-521.

Keller, Rosemary Skinner. "New England Women: Ideology and Experience in First Generation Puritanism 1630-1650." Women and Religion in America. Vol. 2. op. cit. 132-192.

Lofland, John and Stark, Rodney. "Becoming a World Saver: A Theory of Conversion to a Deviant Perspective." American Sociological Review. 30 (1965) : 862-875.

Miller, Char. ed. "Teach Me O My God: The Journal of Hiram Bingham (1815-1816)." Vermont History. 48 (1980) : 225-235.

Morgan, Edmund S. "The Puritan Ethic and the American Revolution." American Quarterly. XXIV (1967) : 3-43.

Salisbury, Neal. "Red Puritans: The "Praying Indians" of Massachusetts Bay and John Eliot." William and Mary Quarterly. XXXI (1974) 27-54.

Schmotter, James W. "Ministerial Careers in Eighteenth-Century New England: The Social Context 1700-1760." Journal of Social History. 9 (1975) : 249-267.

Smith-Rosenberg, Carroll. "The Female World of Love and Ritual." Signs. 1 (1975) : 1-29.

Sweet, Douglas H. "Church Vitality and the American Revolution: Historiographic Consensus and Thoughts Toward a New Perspective." Church History. 45 (1976) : 341-357.

White, Hayden. "The Forms of Wildness: Archæology of an Idea." The Wild Man Within: An Image of Western Thought from the Renaissance to Romanticism. Dudley, Edward and Novak, Maximillian E. eds. Pittsburgh PA: University of Pittsburgh Press. 1972.

Young, Chester Raymond. "American Missionary Influence on the Union of Church and State in Hawaii During the Regency of Kaahumanu." A Journal of Church and State. IX (1967) : 165-179.

Zuckerman, Michael. "Pilgrims in the Wilderness: Community, Modernity and the Maypole at Merry Mount." New England Quarterly. 50 (1977) : 255-277.

Secondary Sources - Monographs

Ahlstrom, Sydney E. A Religious History of the American People. Vol. 1. Garden City NY: Image Books. 1975.

Ames, Edward Scribner. The Psychology of Religious Experience. New York: Houghton Mifflin Company. 1910.

Allport, Gordon W. Becoming: Basic Considerations for a Psychology of Personality. New Haven MA: Yale University Press. 1955.

Allport, Gordon W. The Individual and His Religion. New York: Macmillan Company. 1950.

Andrew, John A., III. Rebuilding the Christian Commonwealth: New England Congregationalists and Foreign Missions 1800-1830. Lexington: The University Press of Kentucky. 1976.

Axtell, James. The European and the Indian: Essays in the Ethnohistory of Colonial North America. New York: Oxford University Press. 1981.

Baudet, Henri. Paradise on Earth: Some Thoughts on European Images of Non-European Man. New Haven MA: Yale University Press. 1965.

Benson, Mary Sumner. Women in the Eighteenth Century. 1935. Reprint, Port Washington NY: Kennikat Press, Inc. 1966.

Bercovitch, Sacvan. The American Jeremiad. Madison WI: University of Wisconsin Press. 1978.

Berk, Stephen E. Calvinism versus Democracy: Timothy Dwight and the Origins of American Evangelical Orthodoxy. Hamden CT: Archon Books. 1974.

Berkhofer, Robert F., Jr. Salvation and the Savage: An Analysis of Protestant Missions and American Indian Response 1787-1862. New York: Athenium. 1972.

Bodo, John R. The Protestant Clergy and Public Issues 1812-1848. Princeton NJ: Princeton University Press. 1954.

Bradley, Harold Whitman. The American Frontier in Hawaii: The Pioneers 1789-1843. 1942. Reprint, Gloucester MA: Peter Smith. 1968.

Brumberg, Joan Jacobs. Mission for Life: The Story of the Family of Adoniram Judson. New York: Free Press. 1980.

Clark, Elmer T. The Psychology of Religious Awakening. New York: The Macmillan Company. 1929.

Conforti, Joseph A. Samuel Hopkins and the New Divinity Movement. Grand Rapids MI: Christian University Press. 1981.

216

Cowing, Cedric B. The Great Awakening and the American Revolution: Colonial Thought in the Eighteenth Century. Chicago: Rand McNally. 1971.

Cunningham, Charles. Timothy Dwight. New York: The MacMillan Company. 1942.

Davenport, Frederick Morgan. Primitive Traits in Religious Revivals. New York: The MacMillan Company. 1905.

Davidson, James West. The Logic of Millennial Thought: Eighteenth-Century New England. New Haven CT: Yale University Press. 1977.

Daws, Gavan. Shoal of Time. Honolulu: University of Hawaii Press. 1982.

Degler, Carl N. At Odds: Women and the Family in America. New York: Oxford University Press. 1980.

DeJong, James A. As the Waters Cover the Sea: Millennial Expectations in the Rise of Anglo-American Missions 1640-1810. Kampen: J. H. Kok. 1970.

Demos, John. A Little Commonwealth: Family Life in Plymouth Colony. New York: Oxford University Press. 1970.

Dening, Greg. Islands and Beaches. Melbourne, Australia: Melbourne University Press. 1980.

DeSanctus, Sante. Religious Conversion:A Bio-Psychological Study. New York: Harcourt, Brace & Company, Inc. 1927.

Elsbree, Oliver Wendell. The Rise of the Missionary Spirit in America 1790-1815. 1928. Reprint, Philadelphia: Porcupine Press. 1980.

Epstein, Barbara Leslie. The Politics of Domesticity: Women, Evangelism and Temperance in Nineteenth-Century America. Middletown CT: Wesleyan University Press. 1981.

Erikson, Erik H. Identity and the Life Cycle. New York: International Universities Press. 1959.

Erikson, Erik H. Identity, Youth and Crisis. New York:
W. W. Norton & Company Inc. 1968.

Erikson, Erik H. Life, History and the Historical Moment.
New York: W. W. Norton & Company Inc. 1975.

Erikson, Erik H. Young Man Luther: A Study in
Psychoanalysis and History. New York: W. W. Norton
and Company Inc. 1962.

Foster, Charles I. An Errand of Mercy: The Evangelical
United Front 1790-1837. Chapel Hill NC: The
University of North Carolina Press. 1960.

Foster, Frank Hugh. A Genetic History of the New England
Theology. New York: Russell & Russell Inc. 1963.

French, Thomas. The Missionary Whaleship. New York:
Vintage Press. 1961.

Garrett, John. To Live Among the Stars: Christian Origins
in Oceania. Geneva: World Council of Churches. 1982.

Gaustad, Edwin Scott. The Great Awakening in New England.
New York: Harper & Brothers. 1957.

Goen, Clarence Curtis. Revivalism and Separatism in New
England 1740-1800. New Haven CT: Yale University
Press. 1962.

Greven, Philip. The Protestant Temperament: Patterns of
Child-Rearing, Religious Experience and the Self in
Early America. New York: Alfred A. Knopf. 1977.

Gribben, William. The Churches Militant: The War of 1812
and American Religion. New Haven CT: Yale University
Press. 1973.

Halford, Francis John. Nine Doctors and God. Honolulu:
University of Hawaii Press. 1955.

Hall, David D. The Faithful Shepherd: A History of the
New England Ministry in the Seventeenth Century.
Chapel Hill NC: University of North Carolina Press.
1972.

Hatch, Nathan O. The Sacred Cause of Liberty: Republican
Thought and the Millennium in Revolutionary New
England. New Haven CT: Yale University Press. 1977.

Heimert, Alan and Miller, Perry. eds. The Great Awakening: Documents Illustrating the Crisis and Its Consequences. New York: The Bobbs-Merrill Company, Inc. 1967.

Heimert, Alan. Religion and the American Mind from the Great Awakening to the Revolution. Cambridge MA: Harvard University Press. 1966.

Holbrook, Clyde A. The Ethics of Jonathan Edwards' Morality and Aesthetics. Ann Arbor MI: University of Michigan Press. 1973.

James, William. The Varieties of Religious Experience: A Study in Human Nature. 1902. Reprint, New York: Penguin Books. 1982.

Jones, James W. The Shattered Synthesis: New England Puritanism before the Great Awakening. New Haven CT: Yale University Press. 1973.

Judd, Bernice. Advisor. Missionary Album: Portraits and Biographical Sketches of the American Protestant Missionaries to the Hawaiian Islands. Honolulu: Hawaiian Mission Children's Society. 1969.

Kellaway, William. The New England Company 1649-1776: Missionary Society to the American Indians. London: Longmans, Green and Co. Ltd. 1961.

Keller, Charles Roy. The Second Great Awakening in Connecticut. New Haven CT: Yale University Press. 1942.

Kett, Joseph F. Rites of Passage: Adolescence in America 1790 to the Present. New York: Basic Books, Inc. 1977.

Koskinen, Aarne A. Missionary Influence as a Political Factor in the Pacific Islands. Helsinki. 1953.

Kuykendall, Ralph S. The Hawaiian Kingdom. Vol. 1. Honolulu: University of Hawaii Press. 1978.

Longmore, Diane. Tamate, A King: James Chalmers in New Guinea 1877-1901. Melbourne Australia: Melbourne University Press. 1974.

Latourette, Kenneth Scott. <u>Missions and the American Mind</u>. Indianapolis: National Foundation Press. 1949.

Levinson, Daniel J. <u>The Seasons of a Man's Life</u>. New York: Alfred A. Knopf. 1978.

Loomis, Albertine. <u>Grapes of Canaan</u>. New York: Dodd, Mead & Company. 1951.

Lovejoy, David S. <u>Religious Enthusiasm and the Great Awakening</u>. Englewood Cliffs NJ: Prentice Hall Inc. 1969.

McKenzie, John Grant. <u>Nervous Disorders and Religion: A Study of Souls in the Making</u>. London: George Allen and Unwin Ltd. 1951.

Marty, Martin E. <u>Religion, Awakening and Revolution</u>. McGrath Publishing Co. 1977.

Mead, Sidney E. <u>Nathaniel William Taylor 1786-1858: A Connecticut Liberal</u>. 1942. Reprint, Archon Books. 1967.

Meerloo, Joost A. M. <u>The Rape of the Mind</u>: <u>The Psychology of Thought Control, Menticide and Brainwashing</u>. New York: Grosset & Dunlap. 1961.

Miller, Char. <u>Fathers and Sons: The Bingham Family and the American Mission</u>. Philadelphia: Temple University Press. 1982.

Miller, Perry. <u>Jonathan Edwards</u>. William Sloane Associates Inc. 1949.

Miller, Perry. <u>The Life of the Mind in America</u>. New York: Harcourt, Brace & World Inc. 1965.

Miller, Perry. <u>Nature's Nation</u>. Cambridge MA: The Belknap Press. 1967.

Norton, Mary Beth. <u>Liberty's Daughters</u>. Boston: Little, Brown and Company. 1980.

Oates, Wayne E. <u>The Psychology of Religion</u>. Waco TX: Word Books. 1973.

Phillips, Clifton Jackson. Protestant America and the Pagan World: The First Half Century of the American Board of Commissioners for Foreign Missions 1810-1860. Cambridge MA: Harvard East Asian Monographs. 1969.

Richards, Thomas C. Samuel J. Mills: Missionary Pathfinder, Pioneer and Promoter. Boston: The Pilgrim Press. 1906.

Rooy, Sidney H. The Theology of Missions in the Puritan Tradition. Grand Rapids MI: William B. Eerdmans Publishing Co. 1965.

Rowe, Henry K. History of Andover Theological Seminary. Newton MA: Thomas Todd Company, Printers. 1933.

Sahlins, Marshall. Historical Metaphors and Mythical Realities. Ann Arbor MI: University of Michigan Press. 1981.

Sargant, William. Battle for the Mind: A Physiology of Conversion and Brainwashing. Garden City NJ: Doubleday and Company, Inc. 1957.

Sargant, William. The Mind Possessed: A Physiology of Possession, Mysticism and Faith Healing. New York: J. B. Lippincott Company. 1974.

Silverman, Kenneth. Timothy Dwight. New York: Twayne Publishers Inc. 1969.

Simpson, Alan. Puritanism in Old and New England. Chicago: University of Chicago Press. 1955.

Starbuck, Edwin Diller. The Psychology of Religion: An Empirical Study of the Growth of Religious Consciousness. New York: Charles Scribner's Sons. 1901.

Starr, Edward C. A History of Cornwall, Connecticut. New Haven CT: The Tuttle, Morehouse & Taylor Company. 1926.

Sweet, William Warren. Makers of Christianity From John Cotton to Lyman Abbot. New York: Henry Holt and Company. 1937.

Sweet, William Warren. Religion in the Development of American Culture 1765-1840. New York: Charles Scribner's Sons. 1952.

Tuveson, Ernest Lee. Redeemer Nation: The Idea of the American Millennial Role. Chicago: University of Chicago Press. 1968.

Tyler, Alice F. Freedom's Ferment. 1944. Reprint, New York: Harper & Row. 1962.

Vaughan, Alden T. New England Frontier: Puritans and Indians 1620-1675. Boston: Little, Brown and Company. 1965.

Walker, Williston. Ten New England Leaders. 1901. Reprint, New York: Arno Press. 1969.

Walzer, Michael. The Revolution of the Saints: A Study in the Origins of Radical Politics. Cambridge MA: Harvard University Press. 1965.

Wieman, Henry Nelson and Westcott-Wieman, Regina. Normative Psychology of Religion. New York: Thomas Y. Crowell Company. 1935.

Williston, Samuel. William Richards. Cambridge MA: By the Author. 1938.

Wood, Gordon. The Rising Glory of America 1760-1820. New York: George Braziller. 1971.

Wright, J. Eugene. Erikson: Identity and Religion. New York: Seabury Press. 1982.

INDEX

DISTINGUISHED DISSERTATIONS SERIES